I Am a Bacha Posh

I Am a Bacha Posh

My Life as a Woman Living as a Man in Afghanistan

UKMINA MANOORI

In collaboration with Stéphanie Lebrun

Translated by Peter E. Chianchiano Jr.

Skyhorse Publishing

Skyhorse Publishing books may be purchased in bulk at special discounts for sales promotion, corporate gifts, fund-raising, or educational purposes. Special editions can also be created to specifications. For details, contact the Special Sales Department, Skyhorse Publishing, 307 West 36th Street, 11th Floor, New York, NY 10018 or info@skyhorsepublishing.com.

Skyhorse® and Skyhorse Publishing® are registered trademarks of Skyhorse Publishing, Inc.®, a Delaware corporation.

Visit our website at www.skyhorsepublishing.com.

10 9 8 7 6 5 4 3 2 1

Library of Congress Cataloging-in-Publication Data is available on file.

Cover design by Laura Klynstra
Cover photo credit Thinkstock

Print ISBN: 978-1-62914-681-2
Ebook ISBN: 978-1-63220-001-3

Printed in the United States of America

CONTENTS

FOREWORD

They are called *bacha posh*, literally "girls dressed as boys." At birth, their parents decided this: that their daughter will change appearance, name, and identity. She becomes, in the eyes of everyone, the son of the family. It's an old Afghan tradition that effectively permits families without a son to cross-dress one of their daughters to preserve the honor of the family. In this society, dominated by masculine values, it is frowned upon not to have a son and is overall impractical: a girl cannot work, cannot go out alone to provide for the home, cannot help with manual labor; a girl is a burden. All you need to do is cut her hair short, and she can perform tasks reserved for men. A bacha posh, according to Afghan superstition, may also help ward off bad luck and favor the birth of a boy in the family.

In Afghanistan, thousands of girls must cross-dress starting at a young age. There are no reliable statistics, however. This practice is ongoing and discreet. The parents do not say loud and strong, "This is my daughter—she's a bacha posh!" but rather, "This is my son!" In the villages, they wear the traditional dress of men, the *shalwar kameez,* pants and a long shirt. In Kabul, the capital, they are dressed in jeans and hooded sweatshirts, they play soccer and tennis, they go with their mothers to the bazaar, they defend their little sisters on the playground, they are the men of the family when the fathers are not there. However, who is fooled? Who forgets that underneath the shalwar kameez is a little girl's heart that beats? Close relatives and neighbors play along, too—even religious officials. They do not condemn the parents who make this choice—they even encourage it sometimes—and they do not see any offense to Islam, up to a certain point . . .

At puberty, there is no more question of playing along; at this time, the problem is serious and must be adjusted in a much simpler way: go back to the original plan. Girls must forget the shalwar kameez, wear a *niqab,* go back home, learn the domestic tasks, get ready for marriage and maternity . . . in short, embrace the role intended for women. The *mullah* keeps close watch on the recalcitrant who would like to live in sin, those who lie about their identity. The recalcitrant? The rebels? Those who refuse to become women in the eyes of society because they have had a taste of the men's freedom cannot be renounced. How many of them exist? Still, no statistics, but the subject is taboo.

We want to talk about these women. From the age of twelve, when their families tell them they must wear a dress and a veil, they suffocate just to imagine themselves dressed as such. They grew up as boys, they played with them, went to school, went shopping, they were free like them. And then one day their parents, the district mullah, their relatives, all tell them it's over, all of it. No more tennis training, even if you are the champion of Afghanistan, no more school, even if you had planned on continuing your studies, no more friends, even if you have known them your whole life, no more short hair, no more life without constraints; you will become a woman. For many of these young girls, it is already too late.

Imagine: you are raised as a boy, you grew up with this plan, and then tomorrow someone tells you to dress, move, compose yourself, think, and act like a girl. For some, it is simply impossible. So they cling to this lie they have been living since birth. They go out alone, without a veil, work at their own free will, go to school, and play sports . . . They resist their transforming bodies; they hide their chests. To be a bacha posh is, for them, a way of surviving in a society marked by a conservatism that makes women second-class citizens: deprivation of freedom, violence, and unjust laws. Today, 80 percent of Afghans are still illiterate.

At sixteen years old, the social pressure of the emotional blackmailing becomes too much: "You are offending Allah in cheating your own identity; you bring the shame onto your family." Many give up at this point and abandon with regret their shalwar kameez, their jeans and their tee shirts; they learn to polish their nails, wear makeup and dresses and put on the veil, and sometimes to disappear beneath a *burqa*. But they will never be women like the other women: they will live in the nostalgia of an ideal past; more so than the other women, they will know of the gap that separates the women from the men in Afghanistan since they once lived on the other side. Some also say the trauma will help them in the end: Azita Rafat, a former bacha posh who became a political leader, says that during her childhood as a boy, she developed the strength and independence of mind to dare to put herself forward as a candidate in the elections. And so there are others, those who do not give it up—they persist, refusing to let go of their men's clothing and way of life. They commit the sin to stay disobedient women. They are rare and keep quiet, because they risk their lives. They are driven by their mental strength to transform, to give themselves appearances so masculine that they pass by unnoticed: they become men among men. And in their men's disguise, they defy the authorities.

Ukmina is one of these people. She was born in the mountains of southern Afghanistan, in the vicinity of Khost, near the border of Pakistan—in a Pashtun region where an ethnic group strongly upholds their traditions and codes and where women live closed off beneath their burqas. At her birth, her father decided she would be the son of the family. She grew up playing boys' games with the responsibility to look after her mother and her sister. At puberty, she refused to obey, against her father's will and that of the religious authorities. She thus opened the door to an extraordinary fate. She lived through the war against the Soviets; she ran away into the mountains and helped the *Mujahideen*. She acquired the name Ukmina the Warrior and the eternal respect from the men of her village. At the end of the conflict, it was too late to turn back. Under the Taliban regime, she had to hide herself, but she did not abandon her men's clothing. At the reinstatement of democracy, she took her pilgrim stick and knocked on every door in the villages of her district to convince the women to vindicate their rights. Some years later, drenched in triumph at the Council of the Province of Khost, she shook the hand of President Karzai. Ukmina, illiterate and penniless, tread the soil of New York in March 2012, invited to participate in the presentation of a prestigious award in the presence of Michelle Obama and Hillary Clinton.

The story of Ukmina the Warrior is that of a rebel with a big heart. Thirty years of Afghan history are seen on the face of a woman who wanted to be as free as a man. It is also homage to the courageous, strong, exemplary, and admirable women. Women who refused to be invisible, to carry on behind the walls of their burqas, to submit themselves into the slavery of marriage, to accept the principle of their inferiority. They took the appearance of men to better fight for women's rights. And for that, they pay a high price.

— Stéphanie Lebrun, January 2013

1

FROM KABUL TO NEW YORK

I never liked mirrors. The elevator doors opened, and I couldn't escape seeing my own reflection in front of me; it was impossible to avoid.

Fifty-fourth floor.

My eyes met those of a man without a beard, of a woman without charm. Large stature, powerful jaw line. Me. A pointed nose, thin lips. I moved forward, smiling to reveal my false gold tooth. Its original luster was well tarnished. I needed to change it. My eyes. I never really knew the color of them. Neither blue, nor green, nor brown. *Zarze*, as it is called in the language of my people, Pashto.

Forty-seventh floor.

I stepped back. Age had altered my strength as a man. My lumberjack arms remained, my shepherd legs, the stoutness of a healthy Afghan. What would they think of me, down below? I was intimidated. This rich hotel, this conference filled with important people. It was said that Michelle and Hillary would be there. Mrs. Obama and Mrs. Clinton. It made me laugh, anyway. What was I doing there?

Thirty-fifth floor.

I was wearing a black turban with thin white stripes on my head, and some locks of gray hair had escaped. A beige shalwar kameez, a jacket without sleeves made of gray wool: my men's uniform. Masculine shoes, those of a stranger, of a Westerner. I have dressed this way for nearly forty years, since I decided to be a bacha posh, a woman dressed as a man.

Thirty-first floor.

Was it this outfit that had led me there, to the heart of the US Department of State? Among women from all over the world chosen to receive the award for Most Courageous Women of the World? And to think that three months ago, I had never heard of March 8, Women's Day.

This was all because of Shakila. She came to find me during a seminar at Kabul: "We thought of you, Ukmina. You were chosen to represent Afghanistan. If you want, you can join the delegation that will go to New York for March eighth."

This was in January. I thought about it and agreed. Anything that talks about my people is better than nothing. I had the right to be accompanied, to bring someone of my choice, someone who spoke English. My husband, for example. But I was not married, and no one understood this language in my family. I almost refused the invitation then.

I was scared, I admit. Me, Ukmina, the one who had fought the Russians, the one who shook the hand of President Karzai, all of a sudden, I was returning to my former life: I was just an illiterate peasant from southern Afghanistan. A Pashtun without a destiny. But then I thought about Badgai, who lit up my life; who in her men's garb transgressed the laws, clothing, and fears. And so I got on the plane. But to be honest, I was still nervous.

I was going so far, I told myself; there would be all of these women who had certainly done incredible things in their lives. And me, what was I going to say? I made myself sick with these thoughts. I had a fever for many days before my departure. The plane ride was horrible, a nightmare. It was long, and I could not understand anything. We landed in Washington and then took off again for New York. And then I was there, in the elevator.

Twelfth floor.

A man entered. Western. Handsome in his gray suit. He looked at me, surprised. I saw that he did not know with whom he was dealing. Hello, sir? Hello, madam? He preferred not to choose, smiled timidly, and turned his back to me. In Khost, my province, they called me "uncle" on the street. We say this to mature men. Officially, I am forty-five years old, but I look fifteen years older than that. The story of my life shows in my face; the wrinkles are profound.

Second floor.

I was at the US Department of State! And again I thought about Badgai, the strong and brave woman who had the courage no "true" man ever had. Badgai, who asked King Amanullah for an explanation for the assassination of her two brothers. Badgai, who had come back, sad and proud, with their bodies on her horse. Badgai, the man with a woman's body, the woman at the heart of a man, the light of my life. I dedicated that moment to her.

Ding! Lobby.

The elevator tone brought me back to America. It was terrifying. There were more people there than I had ever seen in my whole life. Women, so many women. All courageous, I suppose. But I did not like them. They talked and laughed so loudly, to the point that I wanted to cover my ears sometimes. And they had this way of dressing . . . nude legs and shoulders and necks. I had never seen this before, neither in my village, obviously, nor in Khost, nor in Kabul, nor in Mecca, nowhere I

4

had ever been until then. The free woman. Was this it, freedom? Giving up your body for all to see?

Freedom, for me, is to be respected. And for this, one must respect others and not impose something on them they do not want to see. These women were doctors, lawyers, engineers who came to speak to me. These women had fulfilled their wants, their talents; these women had transformed their luck of being born in the right place at the right time into a tool. These women had the opportunity to become successful—something that we Afghans could not do. Unless we were cunning, denying a part of ourselves, denying being born female, for example. And for this, we needed courage and sacrifices.

People I did not know introduced me to other people I did not know. They took pictures of me. Listening to their whispers brought me back to being one of the Afghans in the delegation who understood a little English: "They are talking to you, Ukmina. They are calling you Ukmina the Warrior!" Others called to me, "It's you, the Afghan woman dressed as a man!"

Sometimes I would smile, sometimes I would make myself look mean, pressing my lips together while slightly narrowing my eyes, like I had in the elevator earlier in front of the mirror. Women from Iran, Iraq,

5

and Germany asked me questions: Was it common for an Afghan woman to dress as a man? Were there others? Yes, I knew that I was not alone. Some told me: "You are a hero—a heroine!" What were they saying?

I attended to speak about our country, about the status of women, the war, the future. I did not hold back, I wouldn't miss an occasion to retell the mess of the American intervention: "You came into Afghanistan, you brought in your dogs, they came into our homes. We Afghans, we hate dogs, dirty animals that scare the angels and prevent them from visiting us. You did not understand our culture." I am not saying that this is why I didn't win the prize for the Most Courageous Woman of the Year, but it must not have helped! The winner was Afghan, another kind, someone well educated. But I did not regret it. This was my job, I represented my country. I couldn't hide the truth and not say what everyone thinks. This is how I am. This is why I wrote this book. So I could tell the truth about Afghani women.

Because I lived as a man for most of my life, I could do this today. What a paradox! But I was seizing the opportunity. I learned not very long ago that I was the only Afghan to know of such a special fate. In our country, we, the bacha posh, the "women dressed as

6

men," made ourselves discreet. No one could say how many of us there were. We made the choice in a single moment of our lives not to renounce the freedom that our simple masculine clothes give but to risk our lives every single day. I wanted to write this book before I became an old woman or ill, before I was no longer able to remember my life, my special fate. Everyone wanted to know why some Afghan women made this choice. I think that from reading what I am going to recount of my life, they will understand. I want them to talk about us, the Afghans who fight to no longer be ghosts, to come back to the visible world. To no longer hide ourselves under burqas or men's clothing.

2

"YOU WILL BE A BOY, MY GIRL"

I never knew my date of birth. At home, we did not celebrate birthdays. On my identity card, it says I was born in the year 1346[1] on the Iranian solar calendar, the calendar that all Pashtuns use. It's a guess, an approximate date; I do not have a birth certificate, no official documentation that announces my arrival into the world. When I was asked for a form of identity, my mother made up stories: you must have been born around 1346, she would tell me. Give or take two years or so. It was sometime in the spring, that she was sure of. She remembered everything else, for when I came out of her belly, my parents wondered if I was going to survive. They had already lost ten children.

I like my mother's name, Soudiqua, "an honest person" in Pashtu, our language. It's what my mother was: honest, and brave. Her life was like that of all the women here. A life of submission. An orphan, she was married at fifteen years old. In our community,

—————————————
1   The year corresponds to 1968.

a woman without a father and without a brother is a woman without protection: they need a husband as soon as possible. She found my father, fifteen years her senior. He owned land and animals: sheep, goats, cows, donkeys, and a camel. He was one of the richest people in the village, one of the most respected. His large beard was already turning gray; it gave him an elderly look, and, in his spare time, he would sort out neighborhood problems when the villagers would consult him. They were a good match; my mother managed well. She lived in her in-laws' home: a mud-brick farmhouse on the outskirts of the village, surrounded by almond trees. In the center was a well that had been constructed by my grandfather, who is no longer on this earth. Life revolved around this sole source of water until night fell. Then, darkness fell over the home like a starry cover, a lead weight. Electricity never made it to our region, closer to Pakistan than Kabul. In the course of time, the everyday routine had not changed much throughout the centuries.

Three years after their marriage, my parents had a son, my older brother, who is still alive. Then, for ten years, a curse fell over the couple. Seven girls and three boys were born under their roof, among them two sets of twins. None of them survived. The only one who lived longer than one year and overcame all the infant maladies drowned six years later.

My father was a brave man, in his own way. He liked to follow the local customs. Beating his wife was one of them. When the children died at birth, for some weeks or months later, he would take his grief out on my mother and beat her violently. "Your father is cruel," she said to me one day in one of her rare moments of defeat and discouragement. I was seven years old, and I did not understand anything. But I already knew that I didn't want this life, my mother's life. My mother had lost her parents when she was still a child and then her own babies. Her life was summarized by the loss of her loved ones. She hardly ever talked about her suffering—her fate was to suffer, to be quiet—when we would speak of the past, she would brush the air with the back of her hand "Miserable times . . . don't ever look at the past, go toward the future, try to have a good life."

When I lived through the first day, my father immediately knew I was going to survive. He waited a month, and, watching me get bigger and put on weight in unusual proportions, given the poverty of the land, he used this phrase, which changed the course of my life: "You will be a boy, my girl." My mother did not oppose, as she also needed a son. My older brother was already ten years old. My parents needed another boy to help provide for the home, run errands, take care of the animals, work the land, do men's jobs—the jobs they have the right to do. We are Muslim and Pashtun, and there are rules: a woman cannot be seen alone in public; this considerably restricts their range of activities.

From that moment on, by the will of my parents, my family and my neighbors had to consider me like a brother, to forget that I was born a girl, and to call me Hukomkhan, "the man that gives orders," and no more by my birth name, Ukmina. If acquaintances came by the house with presents for a girl, my father would decline and say, "This is my son, and not my daughter." I therefore became Hukomkhan. My father was proud of me. When I was five years old, he put me on his shoulders and walked around the village, making me look like a trophy: I was the long-awaited son. He bought me candy, sweets, chocolate, and beautiful clothes. At eight years old, to reward me for my work, he gave me the most beautiful present that I had ever seen in my life: a bicycle! It was amazing. I got on and admired the way we looked, my bike and me, in a small mirror that I held out at arm's length. My brother patiently taught me to pedal without losing balance. It was not easy to do on the rocky roads near the village. I was happy! Free. I no longer felt the burden of my difference, because I did not see it.

In our district, to state that a girl is a boy was nothing exceptional. In the village, there were about fifteen of us dressed like our brothers, in blue shalwar kameez, a long tunic over pants. There were Jania and Sakina, Matgullah, Geengatta, Sharkhamatha, Kamala, and Mamura. Families without sons and without descendants have the right to cross-dress one of their daughters to preserve the family's honor. It is also said that this can ward off bad luck for the future children: the bad luck being the birth of a girl. One superstition concealed a more pragmatic reason: to dress a girl as a boy allowed them to help the family, because she could work and bring home money.

Kamala, for example, did not have a brother, but six sisters. It was she who supported the home; she served tea in a shop. Her relatives knew she was a girl, but the customers took her for a boy and found no problem with having their favorite drink served to them by this child whose hair was hidden under a hat and who wore masculine clothing. If Kamala had not made up herself this way, the shop manager would not have hired her: girls did not work—they stayed in the house! Of course, they knew that Kamala was a girl, but because she was disguised this way, the honor was preserved, and all the world was content.

This is an old tradition in Afghanistan. Everyone knows the story of King Habibullah Khan, who reigned from 1901 to 1919: he modernized the country and brought in Western medicine and initiated many great state reforms. In his palace in Kabul, he had a very modern idea: to guard his harem, he designated one of his daughters to dress in the clothing of a man. Before, there were eunuchs, emasculated and harmless men to look after the women of the emir. He devised a new plan. What's better than a woman to look after other women? And what's better than a man's uniform to direct with authority the king's mistresses? His youngest daughter therefore took the place of the eunuch until the death of her father, who was killed while out hunting. It is said that afterward, she refused to go back to wearing women's clothing and ran away under the identity of a man. Nobody ever heard of her again.

I didn't know if Kamala was happy in her situation. She didn't have the choice to tell the truth; I had the impression that she was of those girls who preferred to keep their hair long to publicize their identities more than hiding it, lying. For me, it was not a problem—quite the opposite! I knew that I was a boy deep down inside my heart, and that the destiny of a man awaited me. I do not lie.

Kamala explained to me one day that I should not get attached to my boy clothes. "When you are ten years old, we will go back to being real girls. My cousin served tea here up until last year, but she is too old now. She wears the veil, and she helps her mother in the house. You will see that you, too, will have to, and you will go back to Ukmina. If not, Allah will punish you, and so will all the mullahs!"

Kamala was right. I knew well that the majority of girls abandon the masculine clothing around ten years old, but I knew a certain Bibi who could help me keep my appearance as a man. She was the same age as my mother, worked at the market, and she had the strength of a man. Word had it that she had killed someone during a fight about land.

When we went to the bazaar, I looked at her out of the corner of my eye. She scared me but also intrigued me. I never dared say a word to her. The villagers call these women *bakri*, a word that means "women without desire," those who give up marriage to stay

15

near to their parents. Nobody here uses the expression bacha posh, a Dari expression, the language of Kabul.

Little girls like me make up part of the landscape: there is no specific name designated for us, no label. We are integrated into the community, even if we have a different life.

At seven years old, when the other girls began to wear a *sadar*, a simple veil only covering the head, we ran in the mud with the boys. My playmates went to school; my father did not see the use in sending me, since I was a girl. I dreamed of learning to read and write. I watched them leave at dawn; I didn't not understand why I couldn't follow them. One night, I took my courage in both hands.

"Father, why do I not have the right to go to school?"

"Because there are no schools for girls."

"But I am not a girl! I work in the fields like the boys, I guard the sheep in the mountains, I play with them . . . so why can I do everything they can except go to school?"

"Because it isn't worth it; you do not need to."

The discussion was over for the day. But I came back to it many times, for weeks and months. I was nine years old when my father made up his mind.

16

He took advantage of a particularly cold winter; the activity of the farm had slowed, and he didn't need me as much.

"Alright, you can go, but only a few days, and you will make up the lost time very quickly. You will be bored and back at the farm—I am sure of it!"

In the district, there were no school for girls, but ten kilometers from the village, there was a public establishment that welcomed boys from the nearby areas. The night before my first day of school, I prepared my most beautiful shalwar kameez, the least damaged of the two that I owned. From the frost-covered window, I caught a glimpse of the sky, illuminated by millions of stars. The day would be cool, but beautiful. My father had come to an agreement with the neighbor that, when their son passed by, he would take me with him. His name was Manirula, like my grandfather. I liked him; we often went out herding together. He had been going to school since the previous year, and he did not like it. He told me that he wanted to stop going as soon as possible because it bored him. It's always like this—those who have the chance to do something forbidden to others do not take advantage of it. . . . He did not realize that, for the last year, I watched him

17

leave every morning with envy. Today, I watched him as he passed through the door of his house and made his way toward mine. I hurried to meet him.

"*Salam alaikum*, Manirula!"

"*Alaikum salam*. So you did it? You convinced your father? You really are the most stubborn person that I know, Hukomkhan!" He was smiling while he said this. I knew that he liked me; we grew up together. I knew that there was no difference between us, between boys and me. He always called me Hukomkhan even though he knew that I was Ukmina, a girl dressed as a boy. Was appearance more important than the truth? Without doubt: because I resembled the other boys, because I did everything to be like them, I was one of them.

That morning I was proud as we took the path to school. The sun rose timidly behind the mountains. We had to walk an hour and a half at a good pace: we kicked rocks; he sent his flying the farthest. When we arrived in front of the little building that housed the classes, I barely noticed time had passed. I stayed close to Manirula in the class; there were about thirty of us, and I sat by his side on a bench. The others did not pay any attention to me. I did not seem like a girl—the honor was preserved; this was not a problem for anyone. The air was ice cold, there was no heating, but I concentrated on the teacher, who taught us how to count while drawing the numbers on the blackboard. Then it was break time, and he came over to me

"You are new—where do you come from?"

"From Dragai."

He looked at me for a long time. He understood. He asked me my first name. I told him,

"Ukmina. But I am called Hukomkhan."

He smiled.

"Welcome, Hukomkhan. But do not give me orders; it is me who makes the rules!"

I liked school; I really wanted to know how to read and write. There, I came close to that which separated the men from the women in our country: education. Men have the right to learn. I did not understand why this right was refused to girls, why there were so few schools for them. Later, these boys would become men, and they would make it their duty to prevent women from accessing this knowledge. Why should women learn to read, when it would only pervert their minds? Why would they need to write, if only to tell nonsense? And the Pashtun men argued that they must protect the women, to make them respectable. They prohibited them from showing themselves, especially in public places, like schools.

My mother encouraged me. Every night she made me recount my day at school. She thought about circumventing my terrible fate as a woman. To make a son out of me was to give me the best chances in her eyes: to be educated. But she could not oppose my father. A few weeks later, he forbade me to return to school; it was spring, and there was too much to do in our fields.

I went back to the way of the pastures. My days started early, at the break of dawn, around 5:00 a.m. After morning prayers, I took the animals out. I met with other children in the village, and we left to spend the day grazing the sheep and cows in the desert or in the mountains, depending on the season. I preferred the mountains; the view was splendid, and we busied ourselves collecting firewood. It was a big responsibility for me to look after the animals, and I dreamed of having a weapon, like the men! In the home of Pashtuns, weapons are for men as jewelry is for women. I chose my faction: I hate jewelry, and I love weapons. As a little girl, I dreamt of pistols and rifles, daggers and sabers. I had no intention of using them, but, in my head as a child, it was the definition of a man! While waiting, I had only a poor stick. I came back at dusk to help my father and brother with different tasks: take out the feed, milk the cows, fix the fence—outdoor and physical work that girls do not do. In the winter, I wove wool, a task reserved for men.

When it rained or when we came back early from the fields, we sometimes had time to play. They were still children, boys and girls mixed, but already they had different games. The girls played *tookay*, jacks, *haki baki*, and hide-and-go-seek. The boys pushed each other to make each other fall down; it was *khusay*, the game of the little cow. They also enjoyed *mardakay*, a kind of marble game, except that we didn't have marbles in our remote, timeless province, so we rolled around little stones by pushing them around with a finger. And, of course, we played soccer. I liked the boys' games; it's with them I spent all my free time.

Every Friday, after the big prayer, we met around the dams. There were plenty of them—the villages dug vast trenches in the soil to hold the rainwater. In the dry season, these reservoirs of water kept the villages alive: the oxen went there to bathe themselves, the women went there to fill their buckets for the kitchen and the laundry, and we went there to bathe and to

21

swim. These were our swimming pools, our lakes, and our joys. It was always a good time there! I swam in these farming waters; I hung from a large piece of wood that served as a raft for us. We held on tight to it; we came back to it with large bursts of children's laughter.

At ten years old, everything changed. Around the lake, the girls and the boys could no longer mix. The body could be glimpsed through wet clothes. My brother and my father forbade me to join the boys.

I did not understand the reason for this sudden rule, and I refused to obey. But my friends knew I was a girl. If I continued to be around them, they would denounce me, because in doing so, I would bring shame on them.

In contrast, in the pastures, far from the world of the adults, they continued to let me play their games with them. I therefore built myself in the ambiguity of my kind. In the eyes of my parents, I was a boy, but I had to stay a girl in the eyes of society: I had to abide by certain rules such as prohibitions. Because I wore men's clothing, I could go out alone in the street or work in the fields; but because my sex was that of a woman, I could

22

not approach the boys. At this age, the other girls veiled themselves. Those who had, like me, lived their childhood as a boy, gave up their shalwar kameez and the freedom that it conferred, little by little. They abandoned their fields and their games to integrate into the framework of their whole life from this point forward: the walls of their home. They learned how to sew, take care of the children, help their mothers. It took a few months before they embraced their destiny as women: at twelve years old, they wore *burqas* and did not leave the house anymore without the presence of a man.

I saw that the gap was widening between the two conditions: the independence and the autonomy that comes with the status of being a man and the confinement and alienation that signifies the life of a woman. In my childhood mind, I did not see anything wrong with envisioning another destiny other than the one I was given by chance at my birth.

For me, there was no doubt that I was a girl, and I accepted that; I couldn't change my nature. But I wanted to live as a man. I worked hard with my parents, I threw myself into doing physical tasks to shape my body, and I exceeded my limits to strengthen my will. Little by little, I felt stronger than the boys around my age and was more courageous than the girls. Because I resisted, I did not bow my head. I hardened myself to face that which did not fail to produce obstacles for me. I had a hunch.

3

IN THE FLESH OF A MAN

"I will never wear a veil."

This is what I told my father, who had just received a visit from the mullah of the village.

"It is a sin to remain dressed as you are. You must become a woman, otherwise we will have problems."

My father became more and more tense, as the pressure of the *ulema*, the religious people of the district, grew more and more every month. *Guna*, a sin. This word penetrated me like a poison arrow. Throughout my childhood, I saw no wrong in wearing boys' clothes, those that my own parents gave me. And now in the eyes of the neighbors, in the eyes of my father, in the eyes of Allah, I was the incarnation of evil.

When I was fifteen years old, I understood that my behavior was anti-Islamic. The mullah I had known since my childhood took me aside. We sat opposite one another on the living room carpet. It was light and pleasant; we all respected him. This was the first time that he had ever addressed me with such firmness.

"Ukmina, listen to me well. Islam does not accept women wearing men's clothing. If a woman does this, she loses her identity and her place in society. A woman has particular emotions because it is a weak creature; it is the contrary for men. You cannot change your name, Ukmina. A woman, by definition, is soft; this is not the case for men. Therefore, when a woman hides herself under men's clothing, she changes herself and becomes a man, and this is outlawed."

"But I want to be free like the men!"

He looked at me, horrified by what I had just said.

"There is no sense in that, Ukmina. A woman cannot gain freedom just by changing her clothing. It is not freedom that she gains, but suffering. She loses her respect and becomes an insult to the society, which insults her in return. Then what do you say, Ukmina? Women are free! They can move about and travel. They need only to be accompanied by their husbands. They can leave the house with a close friend, it is not a problem, and even to go to work, so long as they are accompanied on their journey. You must understand, Ukmina: a woman that wears men's clothing is committing a crime. Islam does not accept this at all."

With that said, he got up and left me alone on my carpet. This speech did nothing to change my determination—quite the contrary. Manirula had said that I was stubborn. Well, I had a reason!

I promised myself I would never give up being faithful to what I was in my heart. My mother needed me; I had to help and protect her. She needed a son and not a daughter. I have a brother and a sister, but my brother was too small to assume the tasks of a man, and my sister could fill the roles of a woman well.

The speech of the mullah had at least made me understand that I was at great risk, but I was courageous, and nothing frightened me. Only my body could betray me, but still everything indicated that I was born to be a man. Unless . . . it was my mind that created this metamorphosis.

At the time, I was tall, much taller than a majority of the girls. My stature was nothing for the boys to be envious of, though. My face is ugly enough to not draw attention to me. I would go out with a turban on my head, a piece of seven-meter long fabric that my father bought and that I wrapped around my skull. The men of the region generally wore a *pakol*—a large wool beret that looks like a cake on top of the head. The commander Massoud would go on to make this famous to the whole world a few years later. I opted for

27

a gray turban with black stripes; it complemented my sand-colored shalwar kameez, which had replaced the blue one I wore as a child. This ensemble became the uniform under which I tied down my budding chest with a tight strip of fabric. Disguised, nobody ever imagined that I was a girl.

My father left to go to the bazaar in Khost, the great city I dreamed of. As a child, it seemed so far away, inaccessible, but with my bike, I got there in less than thirty minutes! The city was dusty and noisy. I loved the liveliness of the streets; on them I saw horses, camels, and cars—until that moment, I had never seen cars before.

To me, the bazaar always seemed to be the center of the world; everything converged there: men met there to chat and smoke some *bidis* (these thin cigarettes that smell like burned earth), anxious women scurried like shadows under their burqas, merchants pushed carts weighed down by mountains of appetizing fruits and vegetables, porters snuck into the crowd loaded with pieces of meat covered in swarms of flies. The disgusting smells mingled with the freshness of herbs; the powdered spices always stung my eyes and made me cough. When I was there, I was drunk with the colors, flavors, and noises, and I felt good.

At my first bazaar, I was comforted that nobody knew me, and when I bought watermelons or grapes, they called me *halaka*, "the boy." I was at the pinnacle of happiness because *halaka* means more than "boy" in Pashto—this literally means "he who is free and moves without restriction." I bought men's clothing for me and women's clothing for my family acquaintances. The neighbors who had known me since my childhood trusted me with this task: they came into Khost only once a year because a man had to accompany them. So, when they needed a piece of fabric for a dress or whatnot, they asked me, the only woman who did not need anyone to take her into town and do the shopping at the bazaar. I was actually able to buy what I wanted; the merchants did not suspect anything. I was free, as free as a man!

In the village, things were not so simple. There were those who officially knew that I was a woman, such as my relatives. There were those who had learned under the seal of confidence, but never talked about it, out of respect to my father. And there were those who listened to the rumors. These are the ones I worried about the most. One evening, when I returned from the pastures with my flock, I passed two girls from the neighboring village. They made fun of me: "You're not a real man, you just changed your clothes!"

I replied, "Stop, you don't know what you're talking about!"

But they continued, and they laughed loudly. I thought they were ugly and stupid. My blood began to boil. I leapt, grabbed them by the hair, and dragged them up to the creek that runs close by. Then I pushed their heads under water. They got away from me and ran away, frightened.

Through this experience, I discovered that violence can take my heart and make me lift mountains. I was stupefied by my reaction: I did not want them to pierce my secret; I certainly did not want them to take me for a half-man. And then I smiled: I had the strength of a man, but I fought like a woman by pulling hair! I still had a lot of progress to make. *One day, I will have a weapon*, I thought. I made this my new oath.

This incident nevertheless changed my relationship with others. I avoided going out; I preferred to stay inside the close circle of those who knew. I became closer to my mother; I was the only one who took care of her, who helped and protected her. Especially against her husband, my father.

I remember one day when I dared, for the first time, to fight him. It was in the middle of the day—he had come home from the fields where he was working for lunch. He knocked at the door so my mother would open it for him. Once, twice: my mother did not hear it; she was cooking. With the third knock, she rushed to the door and was met by my father, whose fists raged across her face. Then he continued his vengeful job with a stick, taking it down on her. She was silent, like a corpse. I arrived then and discovered my father shouting at and beating my mother. I told him to stop, but he didn't listen. So, I grabbed the stick, slapped my father in the face, and grabbed him by the beard. He left his prey and turned toward me, continuing his rage. But I ran faster than him and escaped. I was fifteen years old, and I had just fought my father.

Would a son defend his mother like this? Impossible! His father would never forgive him; he would be covered in shame. A son takes the side of the father; he may even help to correct his father's wife, his own mother. Never the reverse. But because I am a girl, my father forgave me. It's quite normal: after all, I have the weak heart of a woman. For my mother, I was, on the other hand, the ideal child: I was close with her as a daughter is to her mother, and I had the strength of a boy to help with domestic tasks. The heart of a woman in the body of a man. My mother told me often, "It breaks my heart, but you must marry, so that you have children, a beautiful life." I don't know what a "beautiful life" meant. To have a husband, children, and be part of these invisible people, these groups of wrapped-up women, hidden, concealed, subtracted, and beaten? Is this what she meant?

I preferred to stay as I was. I did not want to sacrifice a part of myself and be alone only to become a *bakri*, an old lady.

I had a secret. When I was afraid of the consequences of my choice, I would dream of Badgai. Since my childhood, I had heard of this woman in the mountains who defied the laws and imposed her will. She was very well known in our district. Even my father spoke of her to me with admiration. Badgai became famous in the time of King Amanullah Khan, the founder of the kingdom of Afghanistan. I loved to make my father tell the story; he even took pleasure in telling the epic story on winter evenings. We sat around him and the wood-burning stove, and my brother and I listened to him with our full attention:

"The Amir Amanullah Khan had led the kingdom since the twenties. He wanted to continue the policy of his father, the King Habibullah, to modernize the country so that he could live like a Westerner. He founded schools in Kabul to teach foreign languages, but he wanted to change too much too quickly and came too close to our traditions: with him, we no longer had the right to several wives, we had to ask permission to marry a girl, and he also wanted our women to be able to leave without a veil! What a lack of respect for them! The Shinwaris, the Pashtuns of the east, led an uprising. Badgai's family belonged to the Shinwaris tribe. Two of her brothers went to Kabul to join the Amanullah army; they never returned. They were captured and executed in Kabul. And do you know what she did? She went to Kabul to ask for the bodies of her assassinated brothers!"

"But how, Father?" I asked him, wide-eyed, the first time he told me this story. "Badgai is a woman!"

"Because Badgai dressed like a man! She wore her brothers' clothes, covered her head with a turban, and took weapons and two horses with her. She went to look for her two nephews, the two sons of her deceased brothers, the children. She traveled through the mountains and deserts with them, day and night, without stopping. At dawn of the third day, she arrived at the king's palace. Only to find that King Amanullah had abdicated. He had fled to Europe! But she was not discouraged; she asked to meet with his successor, Mohammad Nadir Shah, a true king, a defender of our values! He allowed her to speak with him, believe it or not! And he handed over the bodies of her two brothers."

The first time I listened to this story, I was petrified. I believed that I was Badgai. I envisioned myself straddling a white *qategani* horse to go ask for accounts from the king. I would have liked to have her courage, her determination, and to live during this time. My father continued; the respect he had for Badgai was clear. His face, usually so severe, shone.

"She brought home the deceased and bloodied remains strapped on the horses. When she arrived, her clothes were covered in blood, and her hands in gold. The king not only gave her the bodies, but also gave her land near Khost."

Upon her return, Badgai became a hero, for men as well as women. The King Nadir Shah made her one of his interlocutors in the province. She met with the governors and powerful authority figures. The villagers came to speak with her, to ask for help in obtaining admission into an administration or school in the capital. She was a symbolic figure because she was the first woman who dared wear men's clothing and sustain herself for the needs of her family following the murders of her two loving brothers.

34

I found a photo of her: I can guess she had the stature and strength of a man. She was wearing a turban, like me, and a shalwar kameez. Without knowing, I imitated her. When I was a child, she was still living in her village in the mountains, and I promised myself that I would go there one day. *If only I could meet her!* I thought. She could help me with the decision that I was going to make.

In the Pashtun community, Badgai, who was very conservative, demanded respect. It was all a paradox. On horseback, she went and defied the king, and in doing so, she acquired a freedom no other woman ever had before. I understood that, to be free, I had to follow this path: not to clash with the code of beliefs of our tribes, but fight with the weapons of the other sex—bee like a man to escape my destiny as a woman. There was no other choice.

The traditions of Islam ensure that it is not so. We can dress our daughter as a boy and make her do work in the fields like a man, and the religious authorities do not care. Puberty marks the time of separation of the sexes; when the blood flows from our bellies, it draws an impassable red line between childhood and adulthood, between women and men. We must return

35

to our respective roles and travel the path put out for us by Allah.

Allah. I had many conversations with him. Because I was a woman, I could not enter the mosque in the village. I addressed my prayers to Him from the small carpet in my room turned toward the window that, by chance, faced the direction of Mecca. I watched the faraway mountains awaken under the heat of the first rays of sunlight. I could not cheat Him, and I wanted to show myself as I was. Only in this moment, face-to-face with Him, I put a white veil on my turban. My head was covered like a woman. But I did not press my hands to my chest; I put them on my belly. I did not put my feet together, but let them separate gently, like a man. "I do not commit sin," I told Him, "I am honest with You." These little arrangements with religion were not suitable for my father, and even less so with the mullah of the village, who now came every week to speak with him. My father had planned his pilgrimage to Mecca. He wanted the situation resolved before his departure, so that he would not have to suffer the divine judgment. But this was no longer possible for me; it was too late. I had tasted the freedom of men; I saw the other girls my age disappear from the streets, become invisible. I did not want to give up. I would be ashamed to abandon this, to not have the courage to say no. Having lived fifteen years in the flesh of a boy had given me the strength of character to carry on. I did not integrate from my childhood the codes of our Pashtun community as the other girls had; I saw the limits and injustices in them, and I could not accept them. I said to my father: "You chose to make me your son; now it is my choice to stay this way." Fighting erupted, and at the same time, my father felt guilty. Everything was his fault, after all.

We did not speak to each other for a few days. On the eve of his departure to Mecca, he tried one last time: "You are committing a sin, and I am responsible for it. I am going to leave, and I cannot go before God this way. You must go back to your original sex." He went on: "You must dress yourself as a woman, get married, and have children—it cannot be any other way. It is my responsibility; I must tell you this and advise you."

Calmly, I responded, "No thank you, Father. That's very nice on your part. I prefer not to have a husband or children and choose my own life."

He understood then that there was nothing else he could do.

37

"Then promise me that one day you, too, will go to Mecca to wash away our sins."

I promised. Sincerely. One day I would go to Mecca. I think that, in fact, my father wouldn't have liked that I became his true daughter. He made this decision with my mother, after all. They were in need of a son, and I had supported my family more than anyone else: I became the best son.

I was finally at peace. This woman's body was more than a triviality; I knew that I had the determination of a man. I managed to stop my father, after all! From the window in my bedroom, I saw the rammed earth houses of the village, the almond trees drooping, weighed down by their pale pink flowers, the green and golden fields of wheat swept away by a gentle springtime breeze. It was my birth season. My father left for Mecca, and it seemed as though I'd been born again. I was no longer an infant whose fate was decided for her. I was a human being who would build her own destiny.

My nostrils quivered from the fragrance of the garden, taste buds aroused by the smell of the bread my mother was cooling. And so I dreamt. I had plenty of dreams. The first was to learn how to read and write. I wanted to be educated. My father had withdrawn

38

me from school; well . . . I would learn another time! Then, I prayed to have the chance to go to Mecca. And unrelentingly, as a pigeon returning to its master, I thought of Badgai. I promised myself I would be good like her and serve the people and my country.

Filled with my innocence and arrogance, I did not hear in the distance the Russian bombers that would destroy our land, kill us, and end my dream.

4

BEING SIXTEEN YEARS OLD IN THE JIHAD

The soldier peered at me with distrust. His blue eyes, small and cold, moved from my turban to my body, like sharpened blades. He wanted to scare me, but if I grimaced, it was because I was sick; my chest burned, I was suffocating.

Content with his effect, he delivered the final blow: "You cannot pass, Mujahideen!" he said before turning on his heel.

I had just lost my chance to go to Kabul by airplane to be treated at the hospital. I'd just met my first Russian soldier and felt, for the first time, the feeling of hatred. He hated me for what I was—an Afghan; I hated him for what he represented—the invader. To the village, the war was but a wind of rumors. We did not know anything other than that the Soviet army occupied the country. Even in Khost, there was not a shadow of a red battalion.

The doctor in Khost could not do anything more for me: "You need to go to Kabul, Hukomkhan. You have a serious lung infection. In Khost, the hospital has nothing. With the war, the medicine comes in dropper bottles up until here."

I was sixteen years old. The war didn't mean anything to me. All I knew was that the other men had pulled out their weapons, and I still had not! The road to Kabul was too dangerous; the Russians were constantly bombing it.

My father had resigned himself to take the plane with me, but I did not pass through the security check. The soldier blocked my turban. "Mujahideen . . ."

The warriors of the holy war—I saw them. My former comrades, with whom I would play *khusay* and *mardokay*, paraded with their rifles and prepared themselves to join the resistance fighters in the mountains. I envied them.

They would join the troops of commander Hekmatyra, a hero in the region. Before opposing the Russians, he had fought the communist regime of the Afghan prince Daoud Khan with the commander Massoud. They were both Islamists and refused the secular republic of Daoud. "Daoud is a puppet at the hands of the Russians," my father repeated. "He is going to corrupt the country!"

This was not what Mohammed Daoud Khan wanted us to think of him: he kept a distance from

42

the Soviets, and they made him pay for it. A military unit directed by Moscow overthrew Daoud, and he lost his life. A few months later, the Red Army invaded Afghanistan one night in December. The year 1980 began poorly: the winter was one of the most unforgiving in the last decade, but it was nothing in comparison to what awaited us.

So we had to take the road. We were not on horses like Badgai but rather in an old bus that threatened to lose a wheel every time we hit a rut. The frozen earth cracked beneath us and was exposed in holes larger than tombs. Around us, a strange silence hung over the desert plains, imprisoned by the winter. Inside the bus, the atmosphere was heavy with unspoken words and glances lost in the foggy windows. For the first time in my life, I smelled fear. This would not be the last time. Sometimes, from afar, it sounded like a buzzing fly. My hands tensed on the fake leather seats. Nothing happened, but my brain was functioning at full speed, capturing every sound, every smell, every movement, recording, analyzing, and inevitably perceiving every piece of information into a potential danger. And then there was no more doubt. Thirty kilometers from Kabul, we came across a tank with the hammer and sickle on a flag. We feared a random search and anything arbitrary. It passed, a menacing shadow, without stopping. This was even more disturbing.

In Kabul, they were everywhere. The Russian soldiers marched in the streets in groups or by twos; they were at home.

My father said, "*Kafir!*" Infidels, the enemies of Islam.

This feeling would not cease to spread through the country and to me, as well.

For the time being, I was admitted to Musturart, the hospital for women. My father refused to take me to the hospital for men. "They will figure it out very quickly, Ukmina!"

The nurses took off my shalwar kameez and clothed me in patient attire—a long gown. They wanted me to remove my turban, but that was out of the question! It was the first time I was dressed as a woman, and I hated it. When they left, I stripped naked and threw the clothes out the window. After this incident, they put me on the top floor, in a special room for sick people from the tribal area—areas from the east and mostly Pashtun. I was with other women

44

from my community. They didn't want to undress; they were veiled from head to toe. They were perceived as fundamentalists, and in the Democratic Republic of Afghanistan, this is looked down upon. I find myself to be a paradox among them, the woman who refuses to cover herself.

I spent three months at the hospital, healing from my lung infection. When I left, Afghanistan was not the same country anymore.

Khost, this time, was not spared; fights raged on. Upon my return to the village, I found deserted streets: women, children, and elderly people had joined the cohorts of refugees fleeing toward neighboring Pakistan; the men had joined the *jihad* and were hiding in the mountains. My mother was waiting for me. My older brother lived in Khost, and my younger brother and my sister, still children, stayed with my parents. The decision was made to go to the mountains. *If everyone in the country left for Pakistan, who would be left to defend it?* I wondered.

My father decided to go with my mother. My brother, my sister, and I would stay at the house until my father returned. "You will join them with the flock of sheep, my son," my father said. It occurred to me that, had I been a "normal" girl, no one would have guarded the house.

And so they left. They abandoned their farms, their whole lives. A few other villagers stayed, but I felt very much alone.

One night, a group of Mujahideen arrived in the village and knocked on my door. They wanted to eat. I had some flour left, but I did not know how to make bread! I had been doing masonry and grazing the cattle; I had learned nothing in the kitchen. But I tried anyway: three of the four loaves were inedible, hard as a brick, and I burned my hands in the process.

"Make it yourselves!" I said to them. "You are men, and so am I!" This made them laugh, and then they got busy cooking!

A few days later, my father came back. He told me we could no longer stay here at the house and that we must leave. We loaded up a cart, pulled by a donkey, with kitchen utensils, warm clothing, and blankets; we also took ten sheep, a cow, and a camel. I looked at our farm one last time, not knowing I would not see it again for some years. The almond trees were in bloom again; there would be no one to harvest the wheat this year.

The first night, we slept with two other families in a cave. It was wet and cold, and we heard the bombs falling in the distance. The mountains, refuge for the Mujahideen, were constantly the target for the Russian bombers.

The next day, we went back on the goat trail. We were moving with much difficulty, and we had to abandon our cart. We carried the bags on our shoulders and continued walking until nightfall, when we came to our family's camp. This was our new home: a few stone houses and caves occupied by villagers of the plains.

I have no happy memories from this time. I left my childhood in Dragai, the village. Now I wanted to fight, to make myself useful. We brought with us an old Charyee, a Russian rifle, we used to kill predators and protect our herds. I was already at my brother's side with the Mujahideen, defying the Red Army with the Charyee. I awaited the first opportunity to join the fighters. It came sooner than I expected.

One night, the silent encampment woke to the noise of words whispered, not stifled. A group of thirty men, fighters, had arrived to rest for a day. I knew some of them, as they were from my village. Their leader, the commander Mohammed Noorjahan

Akber, came from a neighboring village of ours. I did not close one eye that night, and, at dawn, I took my courage in both hands and said, "Commander, I want to fight with you!"

Despite my great size and my shoulders, I didn't have a beard, and my voice gave me away. In addition, the Mujahideen who originated in my village recognized me. "It's not a good idea for you to accompany us. There are no women in the Mujahideen," he told me, without arrogance. "You are without doubt very brave, but if we are taken down by the government troops, we will be filled with shame because we had enlisted a woman!"

He paused, turned his head toward the valley, and added, "But you can help us in many other ways."

Therefore, I officially entered the jihad! The commander gave me a telescope and, every morning, I went to the top of the mountain to look for incoming Russian convoys. If I saw suspicious movement on the road, I had to let them know by using a mirror. By reflecting the sunlight, I could send signals: one flash of light, one vehicle; two, two vehicles, and so on. Soon I earned a promotion; I became a messenger. I left with my herd, and I went into the mountain. Under my shepherd coat, I hid supplies. The donkey came with me, holding pouches of water underneath its blankets. Two flashes of light from the mirror, one fast and the second longer: the signal that I was in place. Two Mujahideen came to me to retrieve the supplies. Why were there so many precautions when we were in the mountains with all the fighters? Because the mountains were crawling with spies. They were everywhere—among us, the villagers, and the Mujahideen, too. Needing to be suspicious of everyone instilled a permanent sense of mistrust and fear in me. What would happen if someone were to give me away?

Then my missions brought me back to Khost. I would go there—just to the plains with my herd—once a month to look for medicines Then I would get on a bicycle left for me and ride into the bazaar.

One day, the Mujahideen entrusted me with a cassette. I had to bring it to Khost and give it to their contact. On the box, the picture of an *imam* indicated that it was a religious discourse, but, in fact, it was a message of propaganda to encourage the Afghans to take their weapons and wage holy war against the Russian infidels. The tape had been recorded in Pakistan. So I proceeded with my flock, a dagger hidden beneath my clothes. Around a corner, I came across an escort of the Afghan army. We were on opposite sides of a stream.

"Come here, *halaka!*"

Boy, the word that I used to love hearing at the bazaar. But at this creek, it did nothing for me.

"*Zanast!*" I respond. In Dari, this is the word for "woman." It was one of the few words I had ever seen in this language, that of Kabul, because I speak Pashto.

One of the soldiers was Pashtun; he knew me. He spoke to the other in Dari, and, in our language, he asked me to throw my jacket over the stream.

"That is all I can give you."

They could not come near me or search me: I was a woman.

"Tell us where you are going!" the soldier said to me in Pashto.

"I am going to see my brother, in Khost."

"Why do you carry this dagger, then?"

"To protect myself."

They spoke to each other and let me go. But what could they do to a woman? I enjoyed my victory and left without any problems to the cassette.

I took this opportunity to visit my brother. He had been injured in a bombing in Khost. His wife, by his bedside, had lost weight. I remembered her at her wedding, beautiful and round.

"There is nothing left to eat," she said to me. "The bazaar is empty. And everything that I found, I have given to your brother."

My brother was suffering; he looked worn out, but he managed to make me smile and was talking.

"Don't worry, Ukmina."

He called me Ukmina, never Hukomkhan. For him, I was always his little sister.

"My leg will heal, and soon I will go see you up there, and we will all leave for Pakistan. We must leave, Ukmina."

He provide me with some news of the situation. In the mountains, the bombings intensified from week to week, but not much was known. The Russian helicopters flew over the anti-revolutionary villages, scattering bombs and death. The war was now going into its second year.

"They want to end the Mujahideen. I heard they will send the special Russian forces to the border with Pakistan, and they will 'clean' the mountains—that is their word. You cannot stay up there any longer."

I agreed. It was not worth the worry. The conditions were still very bad. But we could not leave Afghanistan for Pakistan because we had nothing. We needed more money to pay for the trip.

I went back to the mountains, where a new mission awaited me: to recover the bodies of the soldiers.

The fight got worse. The Mujahideen launched missiles, deserters from the Afghan army joined them with their weapons, and foreign fighters arrived every day from Pakistan to help the jihad. I did not understand them. My father said that they spoke Arabic. We suffered heavy losses. I fought from behind my telescope, because I still did not have the right to participate, while my little brother was now up front with the Mujahideens.

One day, a group from our hometown had just attacked a Russian convoy. I was two kilometers from the battle that followed the attack. When the shooting stopped, I went down to the group of villagers' leader to retrieve the body. The bombings continued. I recognized Gulbatcha and Zarwalikhan. They were eighteen or nineteen years old, my age. I remembered them from when we played soccer together. Gulbatchal was a very good player. He wanted to go to Kabul to play professionally. Zarwalikhan, he was a magician. He could do anything with his hands. He made fun and complicated wooden toys for the children, with pulleys and wheels. He was very nice and generous; he would have been a good man.

When the Russian helicopters disappeared from the sky, I loaded the two bodies on my camel and rode back to the encampment, where they would be laid to rest with all the respect that was due to them. Gulbatchal and Zarwalikhan were like my brothers. The image of Badgai laying the bodies of her brothers on her horse came to mind. *Ah, Badgai, when will this war end? Will anything of my country remain after this massacre? Who will we be then? What will become of us?*

War does not bring any good. The Mujahideen now spread terror. In the beginning, they only had weapons from the villages—revolvers, shotguns. Little by little, they acquired automatic weapons—rocket and missile launchers. They could kill anyone by mistake or simply as a warning. Mohammed Saebkhan, a neighbor with whom I had played often as a child, remained in the village to protect his family home. The Mujahideen launched a missile against the Russians. The missile fell on his house, taking with it the brave Saebkhan. Elsewhere, an entire family was wiped out by a rocket. The Mujahideen had found that the village was not cooperative enough, and by this attack, they meant to say that they could destroy everything if they saw fit. They also sought the "communists," the Afghans

53

who collaborated with the Russians: military, police officers, public officials—no prisoners. They were to be killed. The Mujahideen spread land mines on the roads, our roads . . .

Sometimes, I closed my eyes in a sort of meditation. I would think: *This is not good. When you kill a communist, you kill five Muslims.* I was relieved not to be involved in the death of innocent people.

I also told myself that women were beautiful creatures of God. Men were cruel. I often asked Allah: "Give me the power of men and the kindness of women."

The Mujahideen finished by entrusting me with a weapon, a Kalashnikov, an old model. I was to defend our encampment, because the Russians had changed strategy: the paramilitary groups were trying to infiltrate and attack the Mujahideen in their mountain refuges.

One night, I had to fire seven or eight bullets. But I didn't hit anything. Obviously, I was not very gifted. I was asked to give back the AK47, but I refused.

Today, I still have the weapons that were with me during this tragic period: a belt of stones (in the beginning, I threw stones at the convoys), a dagger, and the Kalashnikov rifle. With them, I feel like Hukomkhan, "the man who gives orders," and I am respected. I like weapons. Without them, I feel naked, but I do not have blood on my hands.

The Mujahideen took back every village, then the district, and finally Khost. Gorbachev wanted to negotiate with the rebels. The withdrawal of the Russians was announced, and we were able to return home, to find our homes . . . or what remained of them.

5

THE TIME OF HEROES

In the six years following our evacuation of our village, we moved around several times to escape the firing of Russian and Afghan forces. During the winter, we suffered from the cold, but during the day, the sun warmed us a little; I liked to offer my back to its rays, which burned when I sat on a rock keeping lookout. I never got bored of the inspiring landscape that offered itself to me: from the rough stone, to the loss of horizon, it was both hostile and protective, immense, beautiful, sacrificial. It was my country, for which I was ready to die. I could not tell the difference between the noise of propeller blades in the distance and my own hunger. When the sun had set, and the sky turned purple, it was time to go back.

The camp was supplied twice a week. The food parcels arrived on the back of a donkey from Pakistan. The only meal of the day was frugal: bread, lentils, goat milk, and sometimes a little bit of sheep meat. We always had a few cattle, but we kept them, protected them: they were our only wealth and testimony of our past, our other life—which had become more and more distant—the one where we had a farm, livestock, and a pasture. The sadness did not overwhelm me when I thought of it. I did not know what fate had in store for us at the end of the war, if it ever ended.

In the evening, we would wrap ourselves in blankets and animal fur. Unable to make a fire, we would find our way around. I witnessed the births and deaths of babies and the elderly fall asleep to the eternal night. Allah spoke to them—the suffering of the refugee: hunger, cold, the spectacle of their weakness and their helplessness.

My father fell ill. He coughed and spat up blood. He became very weak and could no longer stand up from the straw mattress that served as his bed. We should have gone to Pakistan, to the hospital in Peshawar, which was only 150 kilometers away and closer than the hospital in Kabul. It was also safer because the Russians had not yet left the country: they had retreated to the cities and the strategic sites, leaving the Afghan army to fight against the rebels. But to take my father to the hospital, we would have had to pay a smuggler and travel by donkey, and we did not have the money; my father would not have survived.

So we took the trail to return to Dragai, our village— my mother, my father, my sister, and me. My younger brother stayed with the Mujahideen, my elder brother was still in Khost. I was the man of the family; there was no longer a shadow of doubt. My body continued its metamorphosis. I measured five feet seven inches tall— larger than my father. Life in the mountains caused me to lose weight, but my arms were powerful, and I had strong shoulders. I do not know if it was from wearing men's clothing that little by little any trace of femininity was erased, or if I would have been just as well off regardless of the clothing. Once a month, the blood that escaped my body reminded me of who I was.

One morning, I woke up in the freezing cold, and an unusual agitation was rocking the camp. The rumors were confirmed: Soviet troops were retreating, and the hour of our victory was approaching; it was now possible to think about the future. I entered the war in my adolescence, and I left it at the age when I would have had to be married and have children. This life was getting further than ever from me: to build a family had never been my purpose in life, and the war offered me another destiny. I acquired the decoration of Mujahideen —"who has done the jihad"—a stature that would gain me the respect of others for the rest of my life.

The return was painful. We had to overcome the challenge before us. Everything, absolutely everything, had been destroyed. The Russians had applied the scorched-earth strategy. The villages we passed through had nothing left. The fire had ravaged the buildings, the barns, and the fields. The tanks had crushed the fences and trees and had broken down the roads. The men had completed the work started by armed attack: with shovels, they had blocked the wells.

Our farm was no exception. The roof had burned down; all that remained were the walls. Inside, it had been looted and ransacked. The well was filled with stones, just like the pond where I would swim as a child. But what broke my heart was the sight of the almond trees. There were two hundred of them around our farm before the war; they had chopped down every single one of them. I was wandering around this vegetation cemetery, cursing the war and its lackey soldiers who behaved like rabid dogs, when I saw a thin branch with some fine green leaves. I brought myself to the bedside of this convalescent tree. Life was slipping away from it as a hot and sticky sap, and hope gave me courage. I soon found another survivor, then two, then three . . . nine. Nine almond trees had withstood the onslaught! They would be our rafts to

60

distribute the seeds to sow for the rebirth. Even today, I still have a passion for almonds. Not one day passes that I do not nibble on some of them with a cup of tea. (If you want to get on my good side, give me a nice box filled with almonds!)

We had to rebuild everything, but we had nothing. The first night, we made a shelter from what remained of the house, with the dead wood as a roof. My mother cooked our usual meal: a little bit of bread soaked in goat milk. We snuggled against each other to shield us from the cold so that we could sleep. Sleep did not come—it came to me and then escaped—washed away by the polar air currents. As I did not close an eye that night, I continued to think about this mess. Before the war, we were united and happy in our family. Now we were scattered, sick, and poor. Miserable even. And why? What had we done to the Russians? What had we done to the leaders of our country? I wondered if we would ever learn to live in peace one day, if I would fulfill my dream: to learn how to read and write.

In the morning, I saw the first glimmers of light, blue and fragile. Pale rays trying to impose their light on a dark landscape, without hope. We did not have clean water to drink or to irrigate the fields. At the end of the third day, a tanker truck came to the village, but the water it brought was not free and too expensive for us. We had to swallow brackish and foul water that came from the dirtied wells. We had returned to the eighteenth century.

My elder brother had joined us: he had fled from Khost, which had been taken over by the Russians, who, in a last gasp of pride, wanted to leave Afghanistan on a military victory. He spent all of his savings and bought an old tractor to dig a new well. Life began again, slowly.

To pay for the supplies we needed to reconstruct the well, we sold most of the land for a paltry amount of money, but we had no choice. Those who bought the land from us were returning from Pakistan. The refugees took advantage of their exile. Many of them, upon reentering Peshawar, invested in a tea shop, a small business, and they amassed enough money to consider a brighter future than ours.

They had their hands full, but I felt stronger about other things, and I did not envy them. The rumor that I was "a good person" circulated—that I helped the Mujahideen—and the men and women who returned to the village had great respect for me. Nobody made comments about my choices any more: I was older than twenty, and my body looked like that of a man. My family and my neighbors no longer believed that I would end up as a bakri, an old girl, but rather, as a hero.

My father's heath declined day by day. His coughing fits became more profound and lasted longer. It was as though his soul was leaving his body through his throat. One night, he felt the end was near and made me come over to him.

"Promise me still, Ukmina, that you will go to Mecca. Allah forgives all those who served in the jihad, but if you do the *Hadj*, you will become great in His eyes. I did not sell all of the land. The remaining land is for you. When you are ready, sell it and go see Him."

A few days later, he took his last breath. My mother cried. He had a heavy hand more often than not, but he was a good man. A true Pashtun.

I drowned my sorrow in work on the farm. My brother returned to Khost, which had been recently liberated; this time, the Russians had left for good.

The year 1989 began well, but the victory had a bitter taste: the last Russian soldier left Afghanistan with a souvenir of a million Afghan civilians murdered. Four million refugees fled to Pakistan and would return. Among them were students of religion. Close to the border, I had the privilege of discovering the Taliban, who were teeming as thugs and preparing a bad attack. And of realizing, quickly, that they would not be my friends.

6

PRISONER UNDER THE TALIBAN

In Kabul, the battle raged between the different Mujahideen factions, the warlords shared the country and, during this time, the Taliban arrived in a large mass in Pakistan. Afghanistan, coming out of thirty years of conflict, was drained but still appetizing enough to arouse the lust of men greedy for power. In the village, we were protected from the postwar turmoil, but it was the calm before the storm. I went back to my chores: riding my bike, I regularly went to the bazaar in Khost to buy supplies. And I saw from week to week the misfortune that came over a city that had just regained its color.

I made friends with a *Malang*, a wise man, a bright old man, a poet. He gave me medicine when my back hurt. Years of masonry, working in the fields, and a hard life in the mountains had left their marks on me, and I saw them all the time. The Malang belonged to the sect of Sufis, a branch of the Muslim religion, moderate and spiritual, despised and fought against by the Sunnis, the majority in Afghanistan. The

Pashtuns are Sunni Muslims, the Taliban as well. But I liked this Malang a lot; he treated me and soothed me and I admired the perspective he brought to the world around him, curious and caring. Things were different the last time we met, though—I saw him sitting under his tree, a shadow drowning his face, an omen, his shoulders more arched than usual, seeming to carry the weight of the world. I sat by his side in the Afghan way—crouched, arms laying on the thighs, a position that we practice since childhood and in which we can stay for hours to reflect and meditate.

Here, we are so close to one another; protected by the shade of the tree, we witnessed in silence the spectacle that was before us: Three pickup trucks were parked, or rather stopped, in the middle of the road. On the rear platform, young Taliban members overtook the passengers, who, by reflex, cast their eyes down. Only the Malang and I dared to watch them. After a few minutes, the Malang turned to me and, in a low voice, gave me his diagnosis, assuring that he was not talking about my bad back or my joints: "These are bad people, and they are going to destroy what is left of the country. Unfortunately, for this illness, I do not have a remedy." He took his cane and withdrew with his slow and stiff steps. I never saw him again.

After he left, I stayed only a few meters away from the Taliban. Their long shalwar kameez hung down to their feet, and they boasted heavy beards. Among them, Afghans, Pashtuns who had grown up in the *madrasas* of Pakistan during the war, but also foreigners whose language I did not understand. They also seemed not to be understood anywhere else; they seem disorganized. To me, they looked like puppets serving a cause from a different time. I took the time to understand what was hiding behind this agitation. I listened to the noise that came from the other side of the street, that which hid me from the pickup trucks. I bypassed them and found a quiet place near a small business. The shop was still open, even though it was prayer time; according to the new Taliban rule, the owner should have closed the shop. The owner of the shop tried to explain to them that he had not seen the time and that he would close the shop immediately. Passersby gathered around to watch the scene, none of them flinching, fascinated. The youngest of the Taliban then took a heavy stick and, with all his strength, struck the poor man, who was old enough to be his father. The crowd remained silent, all fixated with counting blows. At the fifteenth hit, the Taliban ceased their work, and the convoy took off to spread their order and terror elsewhere. I was appalled; I told myself that Allah could not allow such acts. But I was more appalled yet by the attitude of the bystanders. They seemed to be willing to accept all the injustices as long as they were not affected. After ten years of war, these religious fanatics appeared to be the ramparts of the chaos. I did not like them. What happened confirmed my hunch.

A few weeks later, I was back in Khost. The city had been transformed, and I did not recognize it anymore. The bazaar I liked so much had become sad and gray. Fleeting looks, blue *chadors* grazing the walls, scurrying like trapped mice; all of the merchants now had beards and closed their doors during prayer hours. In the alleyways, the Taliban went through the crowds and hit the stragglers, violently pushing them to the mosques. Music, now forbidden, took refuge in our heads. In my head, I hummed the tunes of Ahmed Zaher, the most famous Afghan singer. He had managed to join every community with his lyrics: Pashtuns, Tajiks, Hazaras. The Taliban made all of the singers stay quiet. Fortunately, he was no longer of this world to see this disaster.

Dast az talab nadaraam ta kahme man barayaad
Ya taan rasad ba janan ya jaan ze taan barayad

I do not ask for anything so long as my goal is not reached
Maybe my body will hold or end itself by letting go, betraying me

I felt uncomfortable. I looked like a man, certainly, but without the goddamn beard, I was exposed. I could have passed as a young beardless man, but I took the risk. Fear made me paranoid; I thought that the Taliban stared at me longer than the others, that they didn't look at the other people walking by, that they scrutinized me, looked into my innards, that they had discovered the blood that flows between my legs.

My pace increased, and I grazed past the walls; I imagined that one of them stopped me, flipped off my turban with his baton. My hair was short, but not enough. He saw, understood, and called for reinforcement, a prey of choice, something to serve to the people hungry for blood, a woman to correct, a woman who passes herself off as a man. He realizes this is worse than adultery, an insult to Allah, *guna*, a sin; I am a woman to whip, a woman to stone. My head felt as though it was going to explode, and my legs failed beneath me. My labored breathing choked me, and I ran without realizing it.

69

What was I doing? I was mad, I told myself. Who was I? I was Hukomkhan—the one that gives orders—I am a Mujahideen; I fought the Russians while they were sheltered in Pakistan. Who was I? I am Ukmina—the most courageous woman in Afghanistan. I raised my head, fixed my gaze. *Yes, I am looking at you, you the Taliban, because if I look at you, you will think that I am a man.* No woman would dare, so I dare to.

That evening, I returned from Khost in a car that a neighbor suggested that I move from the village. The night fell upon the road. When a flashlight shone on the windshield, we were forced us to stop. A Taliban security post. The wife of the neighbor kept quiet underneath her chador with her head down, as it should be. I sat next to the driver, in my usual attire, shalwar kameez and turban. The flashlight scanned the inside of the passenger compartment and focused on me, on my feet. I wore closed-toe shoes, "Western." I fixed my gaze on the Taliban, but it did not work. The flashlight turned around and its bearer screamed: "This is a woman, and she is dressed as an American!" The worst insult possible; I was in grave danger. My neighbor took things into his own hands. He explained that I was in the jihad, that I was a war hero, that I would fight against the Americans as I fought against the Russians, that I was an admirer of Osama bin Laden, and so on. He gave them some money, and we were off. They had let me go, but I was scared—very scared. These crazy armed men scared me to death! I was fragile, and I knew I could not handle a beating from their sticks or even worse. So I made the decision that I would now avoid going out.

In the village, I calmed down. The Taliban had not yet come this far, but their ideology was spreading and gaining support. The radio, our only connection to the world, incessantly spit out their fanatic speeches, and the rumors spread: the Taliban cut off hands, stoned, and executed people. Fear revealed the most cowardly, and we all know it was best to avoid them.

For the first time in my life, I wondered if I should renounce my appearance and make myself invisible like all the other women hidden behind their blue chadors. I could have died for the sin that I committed each day by offering my face to the light of day. Guna. The word of the mullah who came to see my father woke me at night. I was sweaty, and I shuddered. How many of my neighbors would condemn me? How long would my exploits on behalf of the Mujahideen protect me?

71

Despite this, I decided not to give it up! I could not trap myself in a shroud of blue and pretend to live; I would slowly die. Of shame.

I refused the confinement of the burqa, but I didn't go out any more. I became a prisoner of my condition. Neither man nor woman, I was suspicious to all. One morning, I heard knocking on my door. My stomach turned into knots every time a visitor came by. It had become very rare these days, as everyone lived isolated and left only for the necessities. But I always imagined the worst: that a neighbor would denounce me, and a pickup of armed Taliban would come to my house. But no, when I opened the door, I came nose-to-nose with a burqa, with an invisible.

"Hello, Ukmina."

I did not recognize the voice; the heavy blue fabric muffled the sound. I searched for the face, but all I could make out were two sad, anonymous eyes. I worried—was it a trap?

"Ukmina, it's me, Kamala!"

Kamala? From my childhood? The one who dressed as a boy and served tea in the tea shop? It was her. I quickly made her come inside; it was best not to loiter outdoors. I had not seen Kamala in years; she left the village after marrying somewhere else in the

72

district. She immediately lifted up her burqa and sat down on the carpet. What was she doing here?

"I am visiting the village to see my parents. My father is very ill; there is no doubt that he will soon die. I came here to warn you, because people are talking about you, Ukmina. No one wants any bad for you, but they are concerned. They say that you should wear the burqa and stop pretending to be a man—it has became too dangerous. You risk death if the Taliban take you."

I laughed to reassure her.

"Do not fear, Kamala. They do not scare me. If they come here, I'll kill them. I am stronger than them. Have you not seen my arms?!"

"Stop, Ukmina! You know very well that they have guns; you have no bearing against that."

"But no one will come. Who knows that there is a woman like me here? No one will tell them, I trust my neighbors."

"Today, you cannot trust anyone. My husband, for example, if he knew—but I would never tell him—he would denounce you."

"Why? Is he one of them?"

"No, not really, but he does not like women like you. Like us."

"He married you!"

"Precisely. He saw that I was not a woman like the others, even if I looked like it."

"What do you mean?"

"It's true that we have not seen each other in a very long time, and then the war separated us. You remember, when we were young, we were the same, dressed as boys, but differently. You liked boys' games, and I dreamed of letting my hair grow long and wearing dresses. I was young then, and for me to be dressed like that meant that I was obliged to go and work in that shop. And I hated it, I hated the people. They treated us badly, us children, as if we were their slaves."

She paused, slightly winded. It was as though she had not spoken for months. Perhaps even years.

"After I grew up, my father found me a job in a small grocery store. I was earning money, and the owner trusted me. Little by little, I learned his trade. He rarely came to the store—except to teach me: he taught me to read, you see! I did the accounts and kept the books. It was as if I had become the patroness. I was even going to the supplier, because, dressed as a boy, I could trade with them. Then the war came, and my parents decided to flee to Pakistan. I helped my

74

father, as son of the family, to prepare everything, and during the journey, by donkey, we had to protect my mother and my five sisters. Upon arriving at Peshawar, I was a boy in the eyes of all; I was fifteen years old. And here again, I found work in trade, and I immediately had a lot of responsibility. I liked this. We lived in a refugee camp and I made acquaintances with Shabina, an Afghan woman from Kabul. She was gentle and beautiful like the day. We became friends, and I spent all my free time with her. On Friday, after prayer, we would explore the land around the camp and walk around the bazaar in Peshawar. For two years, my life was a dream, even though we had nothing and we lived miserably. Then, we were able to move into a building in Peshawar. Eight of us slept in one small room, but at least we had a roof. Shabina still slept in a tent with her parents, but we still managed to see each other. And then one night, my father came to me in the store and told me that it was my last day of work.

"'You are eighteen years old; you must get married.'

"I could not believe my ears. I loved my job, I loved my life, I had forgotten that I was a woman and that I needed to get married to a man, share his bed, give him children! I was terrified and ran away. I found Shabina, and I cried all the tears in my body. Shabina knew my secret. She comforted me and told me that this was the destiny of women and that she did not like it either but that her parents had begun talking to her about marriage. I sank. This meant that I would never see her again. We would have husbands at our side and be locked away in our homes. I was mad with grief. Shabina took my hand, and I let myself go against her body. I felt good, I never wanted to leave the warmth of Shabina. Ukmina, I think that I loved her! Have you ever loved, Ukmina?"

"No."

No, I had never loved, and I had never been loved. The warmth that Kamala talked about, I knew only from my mother. But I was fine; I did not search for the contact of another body or complicated feelings. The love of my relatives was enough for me.

"I liked her because, without her, I felt like I was not really living. She caressed my face, and then she told me to leave. She must have felt that our relationship was no longer one of friendship only and that we should stop putting ourselves in danger. We had no other choice. I left knowing that I would never see her again. I went back to my house. I was already less than a shadow of myself. I was like a prisoner being led to the gallows. I knew that I was going to lose everything: my job, my walks with Shabina in the bazaar, my freedom, in fact. I realized that at that moment, I had lived as a free boy and that everything was finished. And what was the life that waited for me? I was panicking; I had not been educated as a girl. I knew how to read and count, but I didn't know how to cook, or prepare tea, or sew. I never imagined touching the body of a man, and I had begun to love the softness of a woman."

I was captivated by her story. I looked at her; her face had not changed. She still had magnificent green almond-shaped eyes, but they no longer had the same light they used to; it was as if the small spark in her eyes had been put out. I imagined her in a *pakol*, a hat, or a turban on her head. She would make a pretty boy.

"A week later, the ceremony took place. I obviously did not know my husband. My father had met him a few weeks earlier. I had not revealed to him that I dressed as a boy, that I was a bacha posh, as they say in Kabul (Shabina is the one who told me this), and that I knew how to read and count. Before the wedding, I was dressed in one of these heavy dresses and adorned with jewelry. I hated it; Each bracelet on each wrist was like a bar in my new prison. I thought it was ridiculous, as if I were disguised. This was it—my life would now be disguised, and I would have to act, to pretend, pretend

77

to be a woman. Nobody can understand this. Ukmina, I am sure you understand this. It's because of this that I wanted to see you. You are lucky; you have been able to stay as such. Me, I do not know anymore who I am. Every time that my husband touches me, it is painful. He feels it. He investigated; it was not difficult to do. He knew where I worked. They spoke about a beautiful young man, and he asked them to describe him—he knew right away. There are girls like us in Pakistan, too, it seems. In any case, because he knew that I only had sisters, he put the story together very quickly. He went to find my father, who admitted to him the truth. Since then, my husband abuses me. He says that I am good for nothing, that I am not worth any more than an animal. Than a dog. It is true—I can't give him a child."

Kamala collapsed; there were not enough rivers to contain her tears. I took her in my arms. There was nothing to say, nothing to do. Girls like us will always be put aside. Girls who have grown up as boys cannot become women like the others, the invisibles who keep silent.

After a long time, Kamala stopped crying. She cleaned up the *kohl* on her face with great skill. She looked at me and smiled.

78

"Thank you. Thank you, Ukmina, I needed this. Since Shabina, I have never trusted another person. It has been years since I have been able to speak my heart, since I have been able to be myself. And you, Ukmina, are you happy to be able to live as a man?"

"I do not know, Kamala. I do not live as a man. As you can see, I am hiding in my home, I avoid going out. You said yourself that I am putting my own life in danger. But I will not change. Only you can understand that it's too late, I cannot do it. I cannot, tomorrow, put on a burqa and go out in the street. I still prefer the prison of my home and my lie, because I am at peace with myself. You said earlier that I am lucky to be still a bacha posh. It's not luck, Kamala—it takes courage. And I do not want to abandon that."

"You are right, Ukmina. I need courage to continue to live this way. We are all courageous, Ukmina. And I am going to continue as well. And I will have children, and my daughters, I will offer them the best education possible so that they can have a life other than the one I had, and I will have the courage to confront their father, who no doubt will be against it. One day, our country will change. Thank you, Ukmina, I will come back to see you. And be careful."

The door closed, and my throat tightened. I was crying. Kamala's story had stirred me; she had taken me back to our childhood, and I was familiar with her suffering. How many times had I imagined what my life would have been like had I followed the will of the mullahs and of my father? I pulled my prayer carpet out, and I knelt down, trembling. I spoke to Allah, and I asked him to bless my father for not having me forcibly married. What a poor wife I would have been! I asked Him for His kindness and His protection for the years to come, because I would not give in. No.

I rolled up my carpet, but I was not yet calm. I lay on my bed and I talked to Badgai, my heroine: she, too, would not give in to the fear and threats. Only she consoled me and allowed me to get some sleep. During these empty hours, I thought about the future: one day, like the English, the Russians, and other invaders, the Taliban would leave. I could then live again and make myself useful. I had wanted to live like a man, but to do what? To be free like them, but I was not. The Taliban referred to me as having a condition of my kind. To fulfill my life, I needed to help women, make the invisible visible. I made this a promise to Badgai.

80

In the meantime, I stayed with my mother. My younger brother had grown up; he was the man of the family now, since I could no longer assume this role. He had the right to go out and work. He accompanied my mother during the rare times that she left the house, for her visits to the doctor especially, because her health was declining. And then she died. A few days later, the Americans bombed Khost.

7

THE FIRST VOTE

2004

We were sitting cross-legged around the carpet where the evening meal was placed. Almonds, dried apricots, tomatoes, meatballs, *kofta*, and rice. It was nearly 7:00 p.m., and I had already plunged my fingers in the dish of lamb with yogurt and grapes. The whole family was together: my two brothers and their wives, my sister and her husband. After the death of my mother, they tried to be around me more. I did not form my own family; I have only them and their children.

The *shorwa* burned our lips, but it was good! My mother gave the recipe for this vegetable soup to my sister; she had a special way of cooking. With every sip, a pang of nostalgia hit me. I missed her.

We spoke very little, absorbed in our thoughts. Even I, usually so chatty, was quiet. The radio was turned on, as it always was during meals, and we listened to it absent-mindedly. It was our only link with the rest of the world. It was 2004, and electricity had still not been restored to the villages of the district. The Pashtun sounds of the provincial radio lull us: prayers and long radio talks about the political situation.

Once the Taliban "officially" left (though they were still there—I'd see them), Hamid Karzai ran the country. Sometimes we heard that he was working with the Americans, but he was a Pashtun, and, for that reason alone, we trusted him. We were tired of war: ten years of Soviet invasion, four years of conflict between the Mujahideen factions, years of anarchy of which the warlords, local mafia, and tyrants took advantage. Six years of Taliban rule, and then the American bombs.

I was lost in all of this, savoring a piece of *Naan je Afghani*, our bread, when all of the sudden my younger brother touched my arm: "Have you heard, Ukmina?"

No, I had not been listening. My ears perked up. According to the voice on the radio, there would soon be an election. We were going to vote twice: once to elect a president and another to choose the members of the parliament, the representatives of the people. The voice uses the word *democracy*, in English. There is no translation for this word in Pashto or Dari. However, we know this word, thanks to the Russians and their "Democratic Party"—not exactly a good memory.

But joy soon took over us. We were all standing around the radio, feeling that a great moment in history was taking place. We had all the reason in the world to feel skeptical, and yet we gave way to hope.

I stayed up late in the night to talk with my brothers and one of my sisters-in-law, and we drank gallons of tea. This was great news, even if we had few details. How was this vote going to work? Could women vote? They had had the right since 1963 but had never had the opportunity to exercise it. Words that had empty meanings for years came back into our discussion: peace, stability, human rights. We wanted to believe that our lives might change.

Shortly after, the census began. Registration offices opened throughout the country to deliver the electoral maps, and all the men and women of voting age were requested to go there.

One morning in the spring of 2004, I left with my two nephews and a few men from the village of Tanai, where the electoral commission in our district was located. We did not have a vehicle, so we walked for a good hour. None of the women of the village went.

The Pashtun women had internalized the principle of the inferiority of their gender, the prohibition to show themselves in public, and to have their picture taken. Moreover, so that it would not offend the Pashtun population, the regulation stipulated that the identity photographs were optional for women.

When we arrived at the registration office, a long line of men blocked us from entering. At the back of the building, women took their turn, out of sight. There were very few of them. Democracy was not socially acceptable. A new word appeared: *amakrasi.* To the Afghan people, this meant: "anyone can do anything." And, by extension, it also meant the emancipation of women. Democracy was Western, and in the West, they did not control their women. But on this day, in my village, they stayed at home.

I made the move, because I am a man! I am part of the visible—it doesn't bother me to have my picture taken. I sensed this was the beginning of a big story for me.

I went to the men's side. When my turn came, I registered myself on the electoral list of men with my birth name, Ukmina. Nobody objected. I had my picture taken: I showed my best smile, showing my two golden teeth. Then I gave my thumbprint in ink. After that, I slid down the side of women to register fifteen villagers who gave me their proxy. They were added to the list, under their husbands' names.

A few weeks later, the officers of the bureau of accreditation came to the village to check the identity of the women who were absent from the registration. And then one day, some other officers brought the cards. This was, I believe, one of the most beautiful days of my life. I held between my hands my first voter card. I wanted to keep it safe and hide it. I put it in a portfolio that I enclosed in a plastic bag and buried it in the garden, under an almond tree. I could not keep the card with me. I did not want to lose it, but it was also dangerous.

The Taliban were no longer hidden. Three years after their defeat, they paraded again through the region. They controlled some roads and stopped vehicles. If they found electoral cards on Afghans, they beat them and ripped up the cards; they saw the cards as symbols of the American enemy. Rumors circulated that they had killed villagers in another district for having these cards. I did not want to take the risk, and when you love something above all, you guard it preciously, no?

October 9, 2004

I remember this day as if it were yesterday. We took the same path to Tanai, with my brothers and my two nephews. This fall day was gentle and calm in appearance. All the authorities of the country were on alert. The Taliban had vowed to sabotage the electoral process, to terrorize the population. Hamid Karzai had recently escaped two assassination attempts.

My whole family voted for him. As good Pashtuns, they still follow the representatives of their tribe. Otherwise, who would give you the money to build hospitals, schools, and roads? It is our conception of the *amakrasi*! I put my left thumb into the indelible blue ink, and then an officer brought me to a poster with the pictures of the eighteen candidates on it. We had to memorize their names. Then we went behind a curtain with a card in hand that contained the same faces. Seventeen men and one woman, Massouda Jala. I did not know who she was, but I was pleased that she was there among them. I put a mark opposite the face of Hamid Karzai and folded the card in half before depositing it in the box.

Some fifty women made this journey; they came to vote, underneath their chador, through another door in the school where the offices were located. I joined them.

THE FIRST VOTE

A certain excitement was spreading. They talked and laughed; some had lifted up the front of their chadors, broad smiles upon their faces. I showed the electoral cards of my sister and my sister-in-law, and I voted for them. They would have come if we had had a vehicle, but the idea of walking an hour on the road stopped them. Other women had been barred by their husbands, who did not want them to show themselves in public. Those who were there had the courage and the slight disarray that reflects the uniqueness of the moment.

On the outside, a festive atmosphere had invaded the court of the school. Some families had come from their village with drums, real wedding orchestras! You could never imagine how happy the people were!

Our hearts filled with hope and pride. On the way back, I realized that the ink had faded; therefore, any fraud was possible. The blue of the democracy, of our first vote, had not held. A bad omen.

The government of Hamid Karzai was very ambitious, especially because they wanted to enforce the new conditions of the Islamic Republic of Afghanistan. Article 22 stipulated that men and women were equal in rights. But between the paper and the reality, there was as much distance as there was from Kabul to America!

In Khost, at the office of the Ministry of Women, Suadiqua explained to me why she had made me come there. She had the same first name as my mother; I concluded immediately that it must also be a "disavowed person," therefore, I listened with attention.

"We have heard about you, and you can help us. You are a free woman, but you are very respected. You can come and go as you wish; you have the ear of men and women. This is what I propose to you: we want to put women in place of the *shuras* in the districts of the provinces. You could take care of Tanai. You must go to every village and every house, to convince the women to take part in these shuras."

The shuras, the village assemblies, are composed exclusively of men. They discuss the problems of the village, neighborhood, land, and of the ongoing projects. My father had been the head of the Shura of Dragi for years.

"I know these women; they do not want to join, and they will not."

"That is what we have to change together, Ukmina. And for this we need you. What is the point of democracy if women do not benefit from it? Do you know what the chairman of Loya Jirga, the parliament in Kabul, said?"

90

I did not know.

"Well, to one of the members who wanted to be heard, he said 'Don't try to put yourself at the same level as men. God did not create you equal to them."

Suadiqua wanted me to react. But I agreed with the sentence!

I replied: "Women and men are not similar. Men are brave and cruel. Women are good and weak. I am brave as a man, and I have the kindness of a woman. I can be cruel if I must, but never low. I will help them at least not suffer the cruelty of men."

I am not sure she really understood where I was coming from, but she seemed relieved to have my accordance.

I got up to leave when she stopped me:

"Ukmina, why do you dress this way? Why did you make the choice to be a bacha posh? Don't you want to have a husband? Children? My sister's daughter was a bacha posh also when she was young, but she has been wearing the clothes of a daughter now for twelve years, and now she has two beautiful boys. And in Kabul, I have a friend who was a bacha posh; she is my age, and it has been a long time since she has worn a shalwar kameez like you! The villagers seem to have accepted this, but the mullahs, do they say anything? And your family, they don't mind it?"

"The mullahs and the villagers, men and women, accept what I am. My family loves me as I am. They know that I am brave. No other bacha posh, as you say, is as brave as me. There were girls like me in my village who dressed themselves as boys, but they all gave it up. Me, I have the courage not to do that."

"But your life, Ukmina? Children?"

"I do not like children. And I have nephews and nieces—that is good enough for me!"

With this, I smiled and left, completely ready for my new job. And it was not easy. You cannot imagine the time and energy that it took. . . .

I knocked on the door of every house and spoke to every woman. I spent about four or five days trying to convince them—them and their husbands. They were not educated, and they did not know how to think for themselves. The first objection concerned security: "If she becomes a member of the shura, it will concern the Taliban."

But we quickly arrived at the heart of the problem: their husbands. They were not prepared to let them go out and into the public, even to the homeless, in their burqas. The names of their wives would be included in a public document, and this—this is not acceptable. *Shame*—the word constantly comes back. The Pashtun traditions do not yield anything for the amakrasi. Quite the opposite! The amakrasi advocated the equality of women—many said this is anarchy and that it must be avoided at all costs.

After four months of never-ending discussions, I lost my voice and gained weight. All over! In each home, I took advantage of the Afghan hospitality. I was greeted with trays of dried fruit: dried dates, apricots, grapes. With almonds—just the sound of the word—I love it! And delicious pastries. We emptied dozens of glasses of tea while talking about the situation of the country, the political and economical problems, foreign soldiers who we thought were really very strange.

I never lost the weight that I gained during those four months, and yet I was walking! I was walking through all the villages in the district. I became even better known. I was Hukomkhan, the man at the heart of a woman, the woman who is as courageous as a man. The men let me enter their homes and talk to their women. The women would listen to me and gave me confidence. And in the end, 150 followed me!

This seems small: 300,656 adults lived in the district of Tanai at that time, and approximately 200,000 of these were women. I think I met every one of them! But I was proud of the 150 women who had braved the eyes of judgment, the threats, and the fear. However, again, I was not finished.

We created three groups, according to the tribes to which they belonged. It is impossible to confuse these three tribes, and you must speak to them separately. Two things nevertheless bring them together: they all wear the burqa, and they all have almost the same problems. After thirty years of war, women were even weaker than before. The conflicts had affected the whole of society, and women in particular. Many of them had lost their husbands—that was probably why they were able to come out! And they had no one to help them. These widows were the dregs of society: without protection, some had come to beg. They were asking for assistance from the government and the international community.

I listened to them patiently. I could not take note of their concerns, because I did not know how to write, but I recorded everything in my head. I encouraged them when they were reluctant to deliver:

"I'm here to listen to you. I will go talk to the government and ask for answers; I will convince them to help you. We will all get out of it. Today we are back, we women; we will rebuild our country, and we will rebuild ourselves."

I spoke to them as equals, and yet I was dressed as a man. But they did not have any problems—they knew that I was one of them. One day, an old woman said to me in front of the entire assembly:

"Thank you for this that you have done for us, Ukmina. You remind me of someone, I must tell you. Have you heard of Badgai?"

I believe that my heart stopped beating for a second. An eternity.

"I know who Badgai is. Have you met her?"

"Yes, she was a brave woman, like you."

"But you saw her—where and when?"

"Oh it was a very long time ago! You were but a child then. She was already old; her face was very wrinkled, and her body was wearing out. She could no longer walk; she spent her days on a wooden chair surrounded by villagers who came to speak to her. Some came from very far to meet her; they asked her to tell her story. And she told them the story of her exploits; she still had a beautiful voice, strong and assured, and her eyes, even at that time, were illuminated."

"Did she seem like an old man or an old woman?"

"She was dressed as a man, with a turban on her head, like you. But with time, I think that nature had resumed its course, and I would say that she made me think of my old mother, except that she still had a lot of charisma. She was wise, an angel, neither man nor woman."

"Do you know if she is still alive?"

She looked at me, surprised.

"If she is still alive, she would be more than one hundred years old, Ukmina. But if you want her to still be alive, you can decide."

Above this, a young voice was heard:

"Now, you are Badgai. Why don't you run for the Council of the Province, Ukmina? If you are elected, you can speak to the people of Khost and even Kabul! Be a candidate, and we will follow you!"

I asked them who would support me. They all raised their hands. I was in the process of becoming Badgai. Like her, I would go meet the authorities of Khost and Kabul, and I would defend the interests of the lesser people, which is what we were.

But before that, I had to fix something with Allah.

8

ALONE BEFORE ALLAH

2006

"Come with me; this year, it is time." It was the third time I had asked my older brother to accompany me to Mecca. I could not go there alone; no woman could go to the holy city without a *moharam sharia*, a close relative, a male escort: a father, a husband, or a brother. I have only my brother.

"We do not have the money, Ukmina."

"We are going to sell the land that our father kept for us to make the pilgrimage. I made that promise, and I must keep it."

"We will go later—these lands are all that we have left."

I understood that argument, but the passion of my youth had given way to guilt; if I did not want to listen to the *mullahs*, I could listen to Allah. I still wore men's clothes, and I was not married; I had not completed my duty as a woman. What must He have thought? I had to explain to Him, so that He might forgive me.

I harassed my brother, and finally his wife convinced him. Faced with two determined women, he eventually succumbed!

"We will go, Ukmina, I promise, in a few months. We will sell the land, and I will settle my debts. I cannot submit to Him when I owe money to my friends. It will take me a little time. But you are right—we must make the Hadj. You must explain yourself to Him. This may be too hard."

"This? But, my brother, what do you mean? 'This,' this is me—this is what I am. I will not change, I just want to kneel before Him and make sure that He understands me and does not judge me. I could only give up my turban if He asked it of me!"

"If you do the Hadj, Ukmina, you must repent to Allah and commit to never revert back to sin."

"Who said that I live in sin? The mullahs? I do not listen to them; I will see Him. He will speak to me, and I will follow Him."

For three months, I prepared. To make the Hadj, you must be in good physical and spiritual condition. You must be able to give anything to the worship of Allah and reflect on the meaning of His way; you must have a sincere intention. I think that there was no one more sincere and motivated than me. I had had an appointment with Him for a long time.

One beautiful morning in September, my brother and I left the house. We would be gone for fifty days.

I lived through this time as though it were a dream. In Khost, we took the bus to Kabul. Looking at the dusty road, I remembered this same journey; I did it with my father at the beginning of the war with the Russians. They were gone, though, and the Americans had taken their place. They were fighting the Taliban just like the Russians had bullied the Mujahideen, and with the same success, it seemed. They wanted to develop the country, but the road was still bumpy, and our district still had no electricity or drinking water. We did not come across tanks but heavy cars marked with a single blue UN. Inside, Westerners wearing bulletproof jackets fixed their gaze in front of them, as if diverting their eyes from our bus might trigger the bomb that we could be carrying. Just like the Russian tanks . . .

In Kabul, we reached the first stage: the Eidgah mosque. All the people taking the Hadj were gathered here for a few days before flying off to Saudi Arabia. We had to change into pilgrim clothes. I bought mine in Khost: long white pants, a kameez, a white dress, an *ehram*, a hijab (a veil), and a shawl, white as well. This was the first time I had put on a dress and a hijab in public. But these clothes do not have the same meaning as in everyday life; these are those of a woman who is presented before Allah, and with Him I must be true. Despite everything, I felt hidden beneath a shroud. I wondered what I would do when I went to Allah. Would I go dressed in three pieces of cloth as a man, or in five pieces of cloth as a woman, including one for the head? Was I going to go bound as a man, or free as a woman? Should I turn my face toward Mecca?

The big day arrived. We left in a group from the parking lot, and we had to walk, passing through multiple security checks. Two hundred meters separated us from the main building, which was protected like a bunker. It took us an hour to get there, but I quickly realized that I was not at the end of the line! At the identity security check, I began to worry. For the trip, I had to have a passport made, for the first time in my life. And on the photo, I was Ukmina with a veil, because it was mandatory for women. I had forgotten this, that I had done that, and it was quite funny. I had gone into a photographer's shop in Khost dressed in a turban with my brother. At first, he put me on the stool facing the photographer, but then my brother had a moment of clarity:

"Ukmina, you must take off your turban; you will have the name Ukmina on your passport, and that is a woman's name—you cannot look like a man!"

I refused at first, but he was right: they could accuse me of having stolen the identity of someone else. I did not have a veil, so the photographer found a piece of fabric to make a hijab that I wore for all of thirty seconds to take the picture. I looked like a big, ugly matron. But this amused the immigration officer, at least. They clearly saw the difference between the man in a turban before them and the woman in the passport photo—I was wearing the white garb of a pilgrim, but I had my turban on top of my head. They spoke in Dari, which I did not understand. The trip organizer came to the rescue, but he was red with anger. I heard my name said many times, Ukmina Manoori. The eyes of the agents passed from my face to the passport, and then they moved toward a small office, followed by the organizer. I remained standing still at the front door. My brother joined me; he was visibly upset, as well. "Why did you wear that bloody turban? I am so used to seeing it that I did not even pay attention to it."

"Me, neither! It doesn't even go well with my outfit today, but I put it on like every other day!"

"They may not let you go through."

"But why? They will see that I am Ukmina Manoori!"

Ten minutes passed, then twenty, and then thirty. My brother went into the office. I was the only one who could prove the truth to them, and nobody wanted to listen to me! The rest of the group had long since passed through security and the checks and had begun boarding. Yet I was not afraid. I rolled the little balls of my prayer beads between my fingers; it calmed me and helped pass the time. I had confidence; Allah was waiting for me, and He knew who I was.

The door opened and the chief of security, followed by three agents, the organizer, and my brother, walked toward me. He handed me the passport without making eye contact and sent me to the line of women, where I was thoroughly searched. "You will never do that again, Ukmina! When you travel, you are wearing a veil from now on!"

I surely did not have luck with planes. I remembered my first aborted trip, when I needed to go to Kabul to heal. The Russian soldier refused my entry at the airport, having taken me for a Mujahideen. This time,

I was suspected of having falsified my identity. The words of the mullah of the village come back to me: "Islam does not allow women who are wearing men's clothes. If a woman does this, she loses her identity and her place in society." Is it that I had lost my identity? My place in society?

When I finally got to my seat on the plane, I asked to be near the window because I wanted to see my country from the sky. Even if I was not very comfortable with my requested arrangement, I did not show it. After the event earlier, I had to make up for it, so I made myself seem like I was very happy. I comforted my brother when the engines shook and the plane soared over the runway. He was clinging to his seat, mumbling a prayer soon resumed by his neighbor and all the others. I did not pray, but I gave myself entirely to the spectacle that offered itself to me.

Kabul was far away now, already more than a collection of confetti in the middle of majestic mountains whose summits are covered in snow. An old Afghan proverb came to mind: "Better is Kabul without gold than Kabul without snow." In our country, where it rains so little, the snow is our only source of water: when it melts, it fills the rivers from which we drink. I could still see a few roads that dug their furrows into the rock, lacing around large stones; from time to time a green stain pointed out a fertile land, and then we were too high and the only things before us were the peaks of the Hindu Kuch, our forest of mountains. I was already elsewhere—I relaxed, I was not afraid, I felt like I had met Him.

And then the dream became reality. Under the belly of the aircraft, the arid plains succeed to the deserts of Saudi Arabia and we landed, among prayers played over the speakers by the captain, on the tarmac at the King Abdulaziz International Airport in Jeddah. Everything was perfectly organized; groups of pilgrims who came from all over the world were directed to air-conditioned buses to travel to the most sacred city of Islam, Mecca, in Bakkah. Seventy kilometers separated us from the holy place of Islam, a place forbidden to non-Muslims.

There were checkpoints along the road. We had to show our identification cards. A non-Muslim who intrudes into Bakkah risks the death penalty or life imprisonment. Our organizer explained all of this to us over the microphone on the bus. I did not wear my turban now; instead I wore the white *hijab*. Was I still a good Muslim? Had I been a sinner since my childhood? What if Allah rejected me?

My doubts faded away as we entered the sacred mosque, Al Masjid al-Haram. I was overwhelmed by the beauty of the Kaaba. I was crying, and I couldn't stop. All the stories I had heard since my childhood about the prophet and the holy places came back to me—Madinah, where Muhammed is buried; the mountain of Arafat, toward which the pilgrims were flocking on the dawn of the second day and where Muhammed made his farewell speech. Here, we prayed until the evening before joining Muzdalifah and spending the night.

I picked up a few stones for the next day. In the morning, I followed the group toward Mina on foot, as one must. Three hundred meters separated us from the place where Abraham took his son Ishmael to sacrifice him. I was overcome by emotions, and, when it was time to lay the rocks at the foot of the three pillars, the place where Iblis (Satan) tried to dissuade Abraham to abandon his son, I cried again.

In front of Him, I prayed, as a woman, hands on my chest. I asked him to accept what I was going to say to Him. I began with a traditional prayer. Then I told Him how happy I was to be here, in this holy place. I asked that He bring peace to my country. And I asked His forgiveness. I spoke to Him about my clothing: "I know that it is not women's clothing. If I am doing something wrong by wearing these clothes, forgive me. If you are not happy with it, you can ask me to change; if it bothers you, I will become someone else. Talk to me; tell me what I must do. If you are angry, send me a sign in my body, something that I can feel, hear, understand, and I will follow your will."

I was quiet then. I concentrated. I was expectant.

Nothing was happening! Allah is great—He had forgiven me! I came to him, open hearted, with honesty, and He told me that I was forgiven.

On the fifth day, I witnessed the fifth pillar of Islam: the sacrifice of hair. Men shave their heads, and women cut their hair very short. I cut mine very short, and I promised myself to never again touch it from that day forth. My hair is long today, but I tie it up every day in my turban. Only I know how much hair I have. And Allah. A sign that, in His eyes, I have not forgotten who I am.

Despite the happiness that I experienced just being there, I was eager to get home. The return journey seemed so long to me, and I had barely set foot in Kabul before I put on my old clothes and got rid of the pilgrim dress. With my shalwar kameez on my back and my turban on my head, I was back in the village with my brother.

And what a welcome! We celebrated the Hadj according to tradition: the villagers lined up to congratulate us; they brought us gifts and garlands of flowers. They all arrived with two garlands in hand, and they were relieved to see that I had not changed. "If you were to return in women's clothing, we would not have been able to hang those flowers around your neck," they said with a big laugh. If I had been dressed as a woman, they could not have approached me to give me the chain of daisy flowers. They seemed pleased to have found Ukmina the Warrior and Hadj Hukomkhan. I had made the jihad and the Hadj; I was now untouchable. Strong in the face of them and Allah, I could now devote myself entirely to my people, to be useful. It was necessary that I continue to accept what the women of the shura had suggested to me: to make democracy a weapon, to make ourselves heard—the poor Afghans nobody had listened to for decades.

The second election in our history was impending. It was to elect representatives to the Council of the Province.

9

CANDIDATE TO SERVE WOMEN

2009

One thousand three hundred votes for Anat Bibi, 1,900 for Zohrah, and 5,464 for Ukmina. I won a seat on the Council of Khost Province, far ahead of the other two candidates running. There would be nine members sitting on the council, including three women. The campaign was fantastic: people encouraged me, and I received plenty of calls from women—and men. Each one said that I was one of them!

I have seen the good and bad that politics can bring—the hope that the voters place in us, but also the corruption and clienteles. Many candidates were rich and spent countless money to buy votes. I did not have any money to waste. The only thing I had been able to do was pay for a driver—only on the day of the election—to transport those who could not get out but wanted to vote for me. And yet I was elected!

A new life had begun for me. I thought of my mother and how I missed her. I would have liked her to have been there; she would have been so proud of me. She wanted a different destiny for her daughter from her own, and she wanted the life of Afghan women changed: the time had come for me to act in this direction.

After the election, I spent the week in Khost. I slept in a small apartment with one of my nephews, who had become my bodyguard. On Thursdays and Fridays, I went back to the village. Each day, we were with the other members of the council from 8:00 a.m. to 4:00 p.m. Anat and Zohrah wore veils, and they expressed some reservations on my presentation in the beginning. I understood that I may have disturbed them. Not only was I dressed as a man, but I behaved like one, as well. I talked with great strength, I had a laugh that could knock you off your feet, and, when I sat down, I did not sit like a delicate woman, legs together to one side and set beneath the body. No, I sat with my thighs apart, or lying on one side; my body was spread long and wide on the mat. I ate like four men; I belched to ease with digestion. Men like my company, as I do not bother them. Elsewhere, the leader of the Council of the Province took things into his own hands. He made a *jirga*, an assembly, to talk about my case. I liked him;

110

he was a good man, and he had an enormous red beard that I envied! He said:

"Islam gives rules, and among these rules there is the fact that nobody can change their identity. Otherwise they risk the punishment of Allah. I know that a member of my female council comes wearing men's clothing. She wears a turban. But she has been this way since her childhood. Her parents were in need of a son. Then she chose to keep this appearance of a man, but there was a war and she defended our country. Then she went to Mecca, and God did not blame her. She is not married; she has paid the price, and that is her choice. Let us love her."

The leader had spoken, the tension receded, and we were able to work together. At 8:00 a.m., the parade began. The inhabitants of the district came to us so that we could help them solve all sorts of problems: disputes about their land, conflicts in the family, etc. They also asked us to intervene for admission to schools, to move to Kabul or elsewhere, to obtain a government-issued driver's license, or even to claim compensation from the US authorities. The last item on that list represented a good half of the complaints: a herd of animals lost during a military operation, a damaged house, a car that had been destroyed . . .

111

We needed to then verify these claims, because the allegations were sometimes whimsical, as they were every time it was possible to get easy money. We asked that the claimant write or have written (a majority of them are illiterate like me) a letter of grievance, which would be recorded by the council; and then we had to take charge of the case and find a solution.

There were several commissions within the shura. I was in charge of women's affairs. I listened for hours to stories and complaints of violent husbands, girls being forcibly married, evil mothers-in-law; widows came begging with their children saying that they did not know what to do. They reminded me of my mother and her suffering; her submission became inevitable. I found them courageous to present themselves as such, to dare to think there may be a solution to their problems and that the solution was located here, within the council. My mother did not have anyone to talk to; women were not represented in assemblies—only men. I was proud to be the ear that heard their confidences. Sometimes my role was simply to give advice; sometimes I intervened with a husband and convinced him to let his wife go to the doctor, for example. And when the case was heavier, I requested the claimant return with a formal letter or figure of his testimony. I wished to be able to write as well, but no. With this letter, though, I could bring the case to the Ministry of Women in Khost; they had the power to trigger the intervention of the police.

Our interventions were delicate because we could not break from the *Pachtunwali*, the code of honor of the Pashtun tribes. Its golden rules: hospitality, courage, and honor. Its consequences: punishment of the guilty, retaliation, and revenge in case of offense, i.e., violence.

I remember a young woman in a village near Khost. She walked two hours under the blazing sun to come to the building that houses the Council of the Province. When she raised the veil of her burqa, her eyes were feverish, her hair stuck to her forehead, and she was out of breath and haggard, like a goat taken from a trap. She had difficulty speaking; she wanted to say so much but could say nothing at all. I could tell she was sick and needed a doctor; she did not need to tell me why she had not seen one earlier. She wanted to protect her husband—protect herself from being punished by her husband—by hiding her identity. He had banned her from getting medical treatment. This case, we gave to the department in Khost; justice was made by the police, and, in the end, the woman was

113

taken care of. Her husband finally came around to understand that he should be committed to *protecting* his wife and children. I visited their village some time later. The family gave me a warm welcome, and everything seemed pleasant. The young woman was doing much better, and she was on her way to healing well. Her husband had stopped the fighting.

Democracy and its assemblies began to change the lives of the Afghan people, especially the Afghan women. Women were able to embrace their rights. I do not know if the brutality, the cruelty, and the savagery of men have declined, but there are now places and people to hear these women who are victims of violence and torture. Today, the perpetrators of abuse now understand that they can go to jail for their acts. However, we are progressing slowly. The traditions are deeply rooted in the Pashtun tribes, and we must take them into account with our interventions. The aim is to avoid the worst: the best will come later.

One day, I received a call from the Ministry of the Women of Khost. "Come—there is a woman in my office who belongs to the Tanai tribe. She said that people in her family wanted to remove her daughters and marry them off forcefully. She fled, and she is sitting in front of me. She said that if nothing is done, she will flee to Kabul, where she could be with only her daughters. Come quickly." When I arrived at Suadiqua's small office, the same office in which I was convinced to bring the women of my district together to form a shura a few years ago, the woman was standing upright—not prostrated. She was a widow. The face of my mother immediately came to me—the orphan who had quickly married someone that she did not know, my father, who was fifteen years older than her.

A woman without protection—that is what this woman was, and her four daughters were suffering the same fate. They were waiting in the adjoining room. The eldest was fifteen years old, looking toward a promising—yet terrible—future. Her sister, who must have been around ten years old, sobbed, and the two younger sisters, seven and four years old, played silently; even the smallest sensed that something serious was happening.

I gently asked the widow: "Who is the man who is supposed to protect you?"

"My uncle," she said in one breath.

I spoke on the phone with the uncle in question.

"It is your responsibility; you must take care of your niece and her daughters. They will spend the night with you: no one should come near them, and, tomorrow, we will settle this."

The uncle reluctantly accepted. Men have a lot of rights and sometimes duties here. When he arrived two hours later, he retrieved the ladies, taking them without a word to the back of a pickup truck, like animals. There is no other comparison.

The following morning, I called the father of the widow to summon him to the council office. I also called her deceased husband's father—he was the one who wanted to marry off the girls. We also asked that a mullah come to give religious insight on the matter, which was primarily motivated by financial issues. After the death of his son, the widow's father-in-law wanted to take the home, but the widow's father wanted his daughter to stay there. Otherwise, where would she go with her daughters? His home! And that was out of the question, for that would make too many mouths to feed! The dealings were made between the two men. The father-in-law finally accepted that the widow remain in the home of his deceased son, on the condition that she gave him her daughters in compensation. The "selling" of the girls for marriage would have brought a comfortable compensation. The thought of this sordid sale had made the widow upset, and she had fled with her four daughters up to Khost. She went to the Ministry of Women, where she clung to her life. Yet the solution that we proposed and that was accepted by everyone will, no doubt, amaze you: the father wanted to take back his daughter, the widow, with him and give her a second marriage, but she needed to sell her daughters to the father-in-law to pay for the wedding and the dowry.

What difference did this make to the widow? In the first case, she would have been alone, without her daughters; in the second, she would still have lost her daughters, but she would have gained the protection of a new home. The widow agreed, and the girls cried. Such is the condition of women—choosing between two evils—but at least now there was a choice. As for the council, we knew that we had avoided the worst: this woman and her four daughters sitting beneath their burqas, begging on a street corner in Kabul, abused, and looked upon as dogs.

Another time, a man came to see us. He asked us for protection because of a dispute with one of his neighbors. The man had come to a conclusion: he wanted a second wife and had promised to exchange his ten-year-old daughter for that of his neighbor, who was in her twenties. The neighbor planned on marrying the ten-year-old girl to his forty-year-old son. But alas, the father of the little girl decided against the trade after marrying the neighbor's daughter. He realized that his daughter was too young to marry a man thirty years older than her. He refused to give her away and therefore had gone back on his word; this was unacceptable to the neighbor—and also forbidden, depending on the local custom. We had to find a solution that not only did not offend the traditions but also protected the child. It was agreed that the father would give his daughter away but that her forty-year-old husband would have to wait until she reached puberty before sharing his bed with her. There were six years left before this occurred, but she would go to her new home, where she would be the maid of her in-laws before becoming their daughter. I went to the village to meet with the girl and to explain the decision to her. Against all expectations, she was satisfied with this because she preferred leaving the house of her father, where her father's new wife, the sister of her future husband, hated her.

These are the stories we had to deal with regularly. I was trying to make my mark, even if it was small, and

I felt that this was only the beginning. Like Badgai, I would bring the word of my people to the leaders of this country. They would be given what was really lacking for them, so they could expand their minds. They needed an education—it always came back to this. The opportunity presented itself more quickly than expected.

10

THE HAND OF PRESIDENT KARZAI

2009

Dawn came, and I finished my prayer. I was recovering slowly; my overweight condition had not improved, and my back made me weaker. I combed my graying hair, which now fell down my back. I wrapped my new turban. In Khost, I bought a new piece of fabric for the occasion—today I had an appointment with the president of the Islamic Republic of Afghanistan, Hamid Karzai. He had been elected for a second term, and he had brought together all the members of the thirty-four provincial councils to Khost. I was very happy but tired: the day before, I had traveled between Khost and Kabul with three other members of the council. I had spent eight hours in the blistering heat in the passenger seat of a car heated by the sun of winter, with the windows closed to keep out the dust, along a terrible road. I was losing hope along the way: Does anyone care about this road? Does anyone care about us, poor Afghans from the mountains? We were in 2009 then, and it had been eight years since NATO troops had been in Afghanistan for peace and development. President Karzai had already escaped several attacks, and the vast majority of the country had not progressed from the Middle Ages. The windshield of the car was full of dust; my back cracked with each pothole. This road would never know the sweetness of bitumen.

There were three hundred of us gathered in the council chamber, waiting for the president. Our group comprised mostly men, though some women were present. I did not know why I mattered. I wondered if I was the only illiterate person there, or if I was the only one who did not speak Dari, the language of Kabul. The room was huge; Persian rugs covered the ground, sofas were arranged all over. The advisers were, naturally, organized by ethnic group; I was with my Pashtun brothers. They felt at home—their voices were more assured and strong; the president is one of them. And then it happened.

Silence.

He gave a sweet and confident smile I had seen before on posters. His white beard was impeccably shaped, its elegance faithful to the reputation of the man. Oddly enough, I did not feel intimidated. In my head, I worried: "What are you doing here, you poor thing! You do not know how to read or write, you come from a village where no one has heard you speak, and you look like a nobody."

But I felt that I had something different compared to those content, fat-bellied barons. Maybe it was because I had an honest vote—I had not bought votes, unlike the majority of these other "elected" officials. I saw what happened in the district at the time of the election: the candidates went around in trucks looking for people to take to vote; they paid them a little fee, and then good news would come from the ballot box. I had never done this; I could not afford it! Even our president, who seemed very clean, had been accused of massive fraud. One third of his votes had been nullified, and there was to be a second round—but, as if by magic, his opponent withdrew. No more second round, and look who we have before us today....

I had discovered politics, and I was fascinated, so I did not miss one bit of his speech. He congratulated us all and talked to us about our responsibility: "You are Afghans, and you represent your community; you must work hard for your people and your country. The people believe in you, you must not deceive them."

123

These were, without doubt, simply words in the air for many, but not for me. I thought about what I would like to bring to the villages: electricity, clean water, an irrigation system for the crops, and schools for girls. I had a letter written about this that I wanted to give to the president.

His speech was finished, and he had begun to shake hands with each council member. Three hundred hands. A handshake, a smile, and a few words for each person. He was my height; he approached me and stopped. He looked at me. "Should I call you my sister or my brother?" This was not what I expected; I had forgotten that I was not a man like the others or a woman like the others.

"You're the president of Afghanistan—whichever you choose, you will be right."

He laughed and said to me: "Okay, my brother!"

He had seen me!

I was so happy; I had wanted him to call me this. I'd chosen to wear these men's clothes forty years ago, and the big day had arrived.

I watched him as he shook hands with these powerful men, hands perfectly manicured, fingers swelling beneath gold rings laced with precious stones. What were they doing to get this power, this money?

Before this, I never thought about becoming involved in politics. But now that I had become a member of the provincial council, yes, I dreamed sometimes. I wanted to go further. I did not want to be a minister but a representative of the people, elected to parliament. Nevertheless, there was a problem: you cannot be a candidate if you are illiterate. Even though I had fought against the Russians, had been elected by my people, had shaken hands with President Karzai, and had listened to Hillary Clinton and Michelle Obama, I was still from a village without education.

I had never been involved in any corrupt affairs or illegal trade, but I did not have the right to enter such an election. My story stopped there. But I would continue to fight for my people in the mountains. I was a symbol to them, a hero, and I would not disappoint them.

Then President Karzai left the conference room, and I made this a new promise to myself.

But what if I were like them, if I had money? It was impossible for me to imagine, because I never would. I was not involved in business like the other politicians were. But if an angel gave me enough money, then I would make sure there was clean water in all of the villages in the district. I would plant trees,

I'd give farmers seeds and fertilizer, and above all, I would assemble a project to improve agriculture: a great irrigation plan. The cost would be about three hundred thousand dollars. It would have to be a very generous angel!

And then I would take care of my own affairs to make sure I would be secure in my old age. Because there is no one to look after me.

With these thoughts in mind, I went back on the road to Khost, on that damned road of stones and dust. I had a job to do. With the Americans.

11

WITH THE AMERICAN TROOPS

2011

I'd been laughing more than usual. They made me laugh, the Americans. They were everywhere in the district. In their tanks, or on foot, weapon at hand, sweating under their bulletproof jackets, they were afraid. The Taliban, ah! The wicked Taliban. They were willing to give anything to eradicate them. But they had spent ten years trying, and the Taliban were still there, and there were even more than before.

The Americans sweat even more under their bulletproof vests, and they yell at us Afghans, who did not ask for any of this. While we were pleased to welcome them in 2001, we had been praying every day for them to leave.

I was on the road to a village in the district, sitting in the rear of a big Japanese car. My driver was at the wheel, and my bodyguard was sitting to my left, right hand raised on a Kalashnikov. I had become someone important, which made me a target, it seemed. My nephew—my younger brother's son—was asleep, with his head on my shoulder. When I was first elected to the Council of the Province, I participated in the amakrasi, so I became the enemy of the Taliban. But rest assured, no one needed to worry about me. I knew everyone in the village—do not show yourself, or I will get you!

The Taliban . . . I saw them wearing shorts, those Taliban! They did not scare me. On principle—and because I like this, I love this, this has not changed—I still had a weapon on me, a Mahkarof Russian pistol. I always had it on hand, especially when I was sleeping. Even during my meetings with the Americans, I had it, because they did not search me anymore!

One morning, I met with a patrol of the Provincial Reconstruction Team (PRT), which I had organized. (That was why they had sent me this big Japanese car—and it was comfortable, I must say. I demanded that my chauffeur drive it. I trusted him.) Negotiating with the PRT was tough.

"I am like you," I told them. "I served in the jihad, and since then I have never been separated from my weapon." I won, as always. They did not have a choice; they needed us. They want to "win hearts and minds." Well, there was work to be done.

I crossed the tenth shielded coalition gate; I tasted metal and dust after every one. They had ruined everything. They had everything in their hands; we were ready to help them. No Afghan could tell the difference between a Russian at the time of the war and an American in the present: it is the old story of the wolf and the dog. For the Afghans, they were similar. They did not have the same appearance, did not use the same methods, but they were doing the same thing. The Russians were more like wolves; they showed their fangs right away. But Afghans hate dogs above all things. They are unclean animals.

A cultural detail that the Americans would not have noticed: when they arrived in the village at night looking for "terrorists," they were screaming like crazy people escaped from an asylum trying to scare everybody, exciting their herd of dogs like Satan bound in hell, and then they let them loose on the houses. Their jaws hanging open, wet with demonic drool, they spread terror, these dogs; it was not enough to escape from their teeth and their deadly claws; they always brought hardship with them. Filthy dogs. Unclean animals.

We arrived. There were about twenty of them. They were sweating. It must be heavy, a bulletproof vest. They took me to a floor inside a small building. I had an appointment with a female delegation of the

PRT. About ten American soldiers were wearing camo and veils on their heads. I laughed. They were wearing veils, and I was not; I still wore my turban. They knew me well now: I was Ukmina, the Afghan who dressed as a man. In the beginning, they were surprised. The translator had introduced me soberly: "This is Ukmina, member of the Council of the Province of Khost." I saw that they had questions, but, professionally, they did not ask me anything.

On our third meeting, one of them dared ask, "Why do you dress like that? We have never seen a woman like you here!"

I responded, "Because I am the bravest woman; the others would not do this—they do not have the courage. I have it for them!"

They quickly realized the advantage that they could get from my presence. They made me go into the villages in the district to meet other women and present their project of reconstruction—they used me in their business seduction. But again, they were completely off the mark! They wanted to give out chickens to the women. This does not spark any enthusiasm at all, but I understood: how do you rebuild a country, such as Afghanistan, by distributing chickens, when we should have roads, water, and electricity! The money

130

was there, but it disappeared in the vast network of corruption that had materialized as the dollars rushed in. What a mess!

We were sitting on sofas around a table. They spoke to me about forming a committee for the women of the district so that they could learn to care for their animals. We spoke for two hours about finding a secure location to host the animals, the women, and the American trainers, but no village chief offered them anything. The translator was mired in the dialog, which rambled on. I had the distinct impression that he had not mastered English and that they did not really understand him. Or he was simply unwilling to comply. In any case, we were not progressing, as usual. I gave my advice: "The chickens, goats, and sheep need to be vaccinated. I know all about this, because I took care of the animals when I was young. We are going to speak about this to women. I can offer you a safe place in my district, Tanai."

I thought briefly about the girls' school.

I paused, and the translator took over. Looking at the faces of the Americans, I felt that it was not very clear to them. "Or, a clinic for women. But they are not going to come to the district office. It is a place for men only—they will never accept going there."

131

The same dazed look. I did not know if this was because of the translator or the content. Sometimes the Americans had difficulty understanding Pashtun women, who refuse to be in a predominantly male place, even when the males are not there. Men have instilled this behavior in them.

"This training can encourage women; that is very good, but look at the problems that are there if you want to help them. Because men already have everything that they need. They can move, work, they have fields, they do what they want. But women, what can they do?"

The translation seemed to be very vague again. We left with the promise of another meeting. I saw their frustration: no doubt that they wanted to help establish peace in this country. They needed to repatriate their dogs. These women all impressed me, in the beginning. The first time that I saw them, with their military camouflage and their guns, I said to myself that if we, too, had the right to put women in the ranks of the Afghan army, it would be a great step forward.

And then one day, they took me with them to Bagram. In a helicopter, I was given the rundown: 17,000 military personnel were in the coalition, of which a large majority were American. There were several airstrips, including a 3,500-meter strip to accommodate a Boeing. There had been an attack from insurgents the previous year, in 2010, and here I was, going into the heart of NATO forces in Afghanistan. Nobody told me about the infamous prison in Bagram, but I had heard the stories. The detainees had been beaten to death by American guards; there was talk of torture and of hundreds of innocent detainees. A few years earlier, in 2008, bibles had been burned. They were found in the prison—bibles that had been translated into Dari and Pashto, sent by an American church. The military chaplain of the American prison was put in charge of converting the detainees. We did not like Americans any more.

They wanted to impress me, my friends in the PRT. It did not bother me, these rows of monstrous aircrafts: the transport aircraft Lockheed C-5 Galaxy, the helicopters with strange names; Chinook, Apache, Black Hawk . . . that was all that I remember. It made me laugh; I was in a good mood. And then I saw them: Afghan women in military attire. I could not believe my eyes! My country had managed to make female soldiers! I do not know how they came to be here. Had they also been bacha posh in their childhood, to dare

133

such a dream, for having the courage and the strength to achieve?

There was then a conference to discuss the place of women in Afghan society: how can we give more of a role to women in the economy? How can we reduce illiteracy and violence against women? A woman named Dawn Liberi, an American, took the floor on behalf of the troops of the coalition: "In a few years, the women of Afghanistan have come a very long way. In 2000, women could not vote, and they were not represented in the government. The violence against women was daily, and accepted by all. Ten years later, Afghan women occupy important positions in different areas: not only in the army, but also in business, education, within the government, and in almost all sectors of human activity."

I thought this was optimistic. This was not precisely what I was noticing every day in the Council of the Province.

There was applause, and then an Afghan woman took the stage, and, from that moment on, she became my new heroine, my other Badgai. She was wearing the green Afghan army uniform, and her chest was adorned with many medals. The American welcomed her by shaking her hand: "And now I give the floor to General Khatol Mohammadzai, the first female parachutist and general of the Afghan army."

I could not believe my ears. I no longer had any desire to laugh; I was looking at her wide-eyed.

Her mouth was animated under the general's hat. An assured voice vibrated through the air, and I was shaking. She smiled. "The first time that I jumped out of a plane, I screamed with all my strength; I thought that the parachute would never open. There was no one to help me, and then the canvas deployed; it pulled forcefully at my shoulders, and I thought I was never going to touch land again. I was lighter than the men, and they were already on the ground, while I was still in the sky. But when I hit the ground, I felt so good that I knew this was what I was supposed to do. I had not told my family, but my mother found out, and she screamed and yelled at me, asking me why I had chosen a profession for men!"

This happened in the 1980s, when the Afghans still believed that women should be like all the other women. Then she talked about the Taliban era, when she could no longer go out and no longer had the right to work with the army, so she sold blankets that she sewed in her home. She had resumed her work with the army under President Karzai and had progressed very well. He appointed her colonel and then general. And she was there, before us.

"These female soldiers (she meant the other Afghan military), those that I saw earlier, can give courage to other women. You say that I am brave, but other Afghan girls are, too; they must be convinced that they are equal to men and that they can do the same things, in all areas.

"To become general, for a woman, particularly in Afghanistan, is not easy. But I worked hard to show the other Afghan women that one of them could also do so. As a paratrooper, because you jump into emptiness, you must be as strong as a storm, you must be like an earthquake, you have with you the energy and determination that could move the world, the universe. That is the image that we must give to ourselves, the paratroopers in the sky—we cannot lie or weaken. And I have accomplished this."

And then, with a big sparkling smile, she concluded:

"I have children. At home, I make them dinner. Inside those walls, I am a woman. Outside, I am a man."

I was crying.

My country had changed. The Taliban did not scare me. When the international troops left, I did not think that there would be chaos as predicted. I had confidence in my country. For the first time in decades, we would be only among ourselves, without invaders or peace fighters. The Taliban would join the government, and then? They would no longer impose their grotesque rules, beatings, or stonings.

This vision was no longer impossible. The unique Afghan army general left the room before I could approach her. I would have liked to speak to her. I realized that it was time: I needed to make a second pilgrimage, to go to where the heroine of my childhood lived, the heroine of my whole life: Badgai.

12

BADGAI, THE SACRIFICE OF THE LIFE
OF A WOMAN

Badgai. I had not stopped thinking about her for more than thirty years.

After attending a wedding near the village where she lived, I decided to travel the distance that separated us. It took me a day to travel across the mountain.

One of my distant cousins was getting married. I had only seen them once before, but in Afghanistan, these ceremonies are used to bring together large families. I would even say that a wedding is considered successful only if there are more than three hundred guests. A thousand would be perfect. There is a kind of competition between the two families: which will offer the greatest hospitality? At this wedding, there were between three hundred and four hundred, so everyone's honor was safe.

I bought some new cloth for my turban and an embroidered waistcoat. My place was on the side with the men; no one doubted this. Because I had gone to Mecca, I had earned respect. They called me uncle, and I heard that some had nicknamed me Ukmina the Warrior, but, without doubt, the children insulted me behind my back and called me bakri, the old girl. I had noticed that I scared them. They saw that something was wrong, but they did not know what.

In Kabul, I passed by unnoticed, but, in some villages, they watched me and laughed, and sometimes they threw stones at me. I couldn't blame them. I thought about a certain old woman dressed in men's clothing who knew my mother in the market. She had frightened me.

I sat down on the carpet beside some people I knew. We talked about the good old times, the jihad, laughing. I was comfortable there; I had the same life as them, I was one of them.

"*As salam alaikum*, Hukomkahn! How are you?"

"*Wa alaikum salam*, Samiullah!"

Samiullah! Tears came to my eyes. My friend from the jihad! I had not seen him in years. "I live in Pakistan now; I just came for the wedding. I am the happy owner of a fabric store in Peshawar! And, Hukomkhan, you have become such a handsome, healthy man."

He touched my round belly and broke out laughing. I also laughed; I must admit—I do have good appetite! We talked about life in the mountains during the war against the Russians. Samiullah had shared the guard shifts with me.

"Do you remember the first time that the Russians sent paratroopers? We did not know what it was! We thought they were big butterflies! When we figured it out, we told the Mujahideen, and they fired at them; when they touched the ground, they were all dead!"

We laughed a lot. You can say that I have a place among these Pashtuns, men who have been through so many conflicts.

The wartime nostalgia was interrupted with music and dance; my neighbor began a typical Pashtun *attan* to the sound of drums, a series of hops from one foot to the other, and then spinning, accompanied by clapping. Samiullah led me; I did a few steps, and then I retired, exhausted! I did not regret coming; I was enjoying myself.

The groom entered, and we greeted him. He looked very elegant in his white shalwar kameez. He joined his bride in the section reserved for women; he was the only one who could enter there—the only one besides me! I accompanied him, because I wanted to take advantage of this privilege: I walk through walls, I am an angel, I come and go across the borders drawn between men and women! There I was on the other side; my cousin welcomed me with a discreet smile: the day of her wedding she should not smile, because it is also a time of sadness, because she will leave her family at the end of the ceremony to join that of her husband. She is beautiful: on top of her hair, which is tied in a bun, is a delicately placed pink hijab, matching her silk dress, which is decorated in shiny pearls.

"Ukmina, my cousin, you at last, you do not go by unnoticed—we recognized you immediately! Are you not jealous when you see these jewels and all these dresses? You do not want to try, just once, to dress like a woman? I am sure that you would look very impressive."

My cousin was teasing me. When I looked at the cloth, the veils, the jewels, I was disgusted. I found this very beautiful on all of these women, but I would rather die than wear them myself. I was wearing two rings, one on each hand. I'd gotten them in Mecca; they were silver with quartz gems, a semi-precious stone reserved for men. A watch on my left wrist was masculine and silver. That was all.

The religious leaders came into the room. They would celebrate the *nikah*, the union. One of them looked at me, and then he diverted his gaze. I was an angel.

The mother of the groom placed a spoonful of henna in the palm of my cousin's hand and covered

142

it with fabric. Then the mother of the bride, my aunt, put the henna on the little finger of her son-in-law and also covered it in a piece of fabric. They were married. I cried like a little girl.

The meal was served, and I found myself again next to Samiullah.

"Let me ask you a question, Hukomkahn. Is this now the women's side?"

He broke out laughing.

"More seriously: Do you do not think that you are missing something—don't you want to put on one of their beautiful dresses?"

"Stop mocking yourself—you know very well that I am no different from you. Would you like to put on one of their beautiful dresses?!"

He laughed again and punched me in the side, like the good old times.

I told him that I came to this wedding because it was near the village where Badgai lived. I talked to him about Badgai for hours when we were on guard in the mountains.

My neighbor heard the conversation and asked me how I knew about Badgai. I told him about my childhood and what role she had played in life, even if I had never met her. He said that I reminded him of her, and that he was from her family and knew her when he was young.

I soon found out that everyone claimed to have a kinship with Badgai. A cousin, a second cousin, a great second cousin. No one could say that they were a direct descendant; Badgai never married and did not have children. Only the two sons of her executed brother could make such a lineage!

Samiullah offered to accompany me. The house where Badgai lived was located away from the village, isolated in a mountain hamlet, twenty minutes from the market.

On the path that led me to her, my heart tightened, and I felt as though I was going to meet a long-lost sister, whom I knew existed for a long time, but who, even though I lived far from her, was so close to me.

I came across a small girl, and her resemblance to Badgai was striking—the same black eyes . . . There are a few photos of Badgai, including the one that I had seen in the governor of Khost's office ten years earlier.

"Hello—do you know where Badgai's house is located?"

"Up the side, at the top, turn left."

"Did you know her?"

144

She looked at me and stared for a moment. She must have thought that I was an old crazy person. And then, being only eight or ten years old, she understood.

"Yes, I knew her very well—she is from my family. Go, she is waiting for you."

Samiullah shrugged his shoulders; he, too, must have thought that I had lost my mind, but he had too much respect for me to deprive me of my dream. At the top of the hill, we turned to the left, and, ten minutes after we'd passed the market, I saw the modest, rammed-earth building. It was inhabited, but nobody came to meet us. When I knocked on the door, I shuddered from head to toe. I was transported into another time, to the space between an instant and an eternity; I hoped that Badgai was still living.

And then I saw her.

There I was, in front of her—and I want to say, Her—with a capital letter. Because like Him, the Great Allah, she had guided my way. She was not at all a small, old, curled-up woman as the woman at the shura had described her to be. She was beautiful and strong; she looked just like the photo. She smiled at me and invited me to have a seat at her side.

A voice interrupted; it was that of the girl from the path. She directed me to the empty seat in front of me:

"She used to sit here. At the end of her life, she could no longer walk."

I watched, dazed. It was as though I had been awakened by a concert of horns. The chair was empty—Badgai was not there.

"She died thirty years ago. She was sick but did not want to be treated; she did not want to leave her village and her people—that is what she said. My mother told me this. The entire village mourned, but not only them. The villagers came from the surrounding area to pay their respects, even the very rich people."

I listened to her, but I did not hear. I approached the chair, and I closed my eyes. I wished that Badgai were still here, in front of me, so she could tell me about her life, about her acts of bravery. I told myself that if she were still alive, she could explain so many things to me, and she would help me, guide me. I was forty years old, but it seemed as though I was only ten. I suddenly felt small between the walls where she had lived. It was as if I realized only then that she had left this world. We would have had so many things to share. I might have asked questions about her trip to Kabul to retrieve the bodies of her brothers, about the kings she had met, about Afghanistan at that time. I would have asked her where and how she learned Dari, the

146

official language of Afghanistan, which I still did not know. I would have talked to her about her choice to wear men's clothing, about how other people viewed it. Had she ever thought to give it up? But I should not ask about intimate issues, not this—that would not do! Personal questions: I do not like them, so I do not know why I would have bothered with this.

I was no longer ten years old, but forty. The age when all women of Afghanistan have suffered enough and wait for death. But not me. I had neither a husband nor children, and you could not possibly know how good it felt! Mostly, because I do not like children. And when I hear some people complain about their children because they do not obey them, it makes me chuckle. Oh, how at peace I am!

I do not have a husband, but why? I know that celibacy is looked upon poorly in our society, but I am fine. I have no one to tell me what I should do or not do, say or not say. Anyway, I have always hated things dealing with love. This is not my nature. Even today, when I look at the television, or movies, or songs, if there is a kiss, I turn my head! I am forty years old, and I act like a ten-year-old, the age when I decided to sacrifice my life to my mother, to help her, to become

a bakri, an old girl. Today my mother is dead, and I
do not regret the sacrifice I made. I was born to live
this life without love or desire, and I am happy with
that. No one has ever said to me "I love you," and I
have never said it to anyone. I do not even know what
word I would use in Pashto to say this. Elsewhere, after
thirty years of war and destruction, I think my people
have lost the meaning and the taste of this word. But
did they ever have it? The conservatism and religious
shackles already left very little room for expressions
of feelings and love. The word is empty—it does not
evoke anything. Our Pashtun poets, however, glorify it.
I even know some verses of "Ghazal de Mirâ," which
became one of the most popular songs of Afghanistan:

> Your breast are apples, your lips are sugar, your
> teeth are pearls; she is everything, my beloved; she
> broke my heart, and that is why I am drowning in
> tears; so sweet, so sweet.
> I owe my services to you; you, think of me, oh
> my love, forever. Morning and night, I sleep in your
> sanctuary; I am your first partner; so sweet, so sweet.

I knew nothing about this kind of love. And if
someone ever said anything like this to me today, I

would smack them across the face! I am not beautiful, and I am old—you can't mock me. It's me who laughs at other people now! I see the surprised look on the faces of those who meet me for the first time, like the Americans in the army, or like all the people who I saw in New York. They wonder if I like women, I'm sure of it.

A French person from an NGO that I knew well once asked me this question in Kabul—that was when I knew that it was possible that other people wondered the same thing. I did not know what she wanted to say, but, apparently, this exists, marriages between women. Between men also, elsewhere in the world. They use the word *lesbian* for women. When she asked me if I was a lesbian, she had to explain to me what it was. I had a look of disgust, because even the thought of contact with another body horrifies me. I cannot— that is all. I have no desire. I finished by saying that I did not know what love was. She laughed: "That is not possible, Ukmina—everyone knows what it is! You are not telling the truth."

She did not want to hear it, so I thought about it and found an example: "Here is my secret: a dog came to visit me one night when I was little, and it bit me; he took out and carried away with him a piece of my flesh, the part of me that housed love and desire. Gone, evaporated, devoured . . . free!"

Now, for the fun of it, I make jokes. I tell the Westerners I meet that I find them beautiful and that I want to marry them under the condition that they convert to Islam. I say this while laughing, looking them straight in the eyes. And I see their discomfort. They are wondering if there is a bit of truth in it. This amuses me so much.

But no, I would never imagine such a thing and permanently offend Allah.

My pleasure is when I walk in the street, and people call me uncle. Here I am Hukomkhan, "the man who gives orders." Here, I feel accomplished, and I say to myself that I have sacrificed nothing. I have done what I had to do. I became what I was. I found my destiny. And there is nothing that I lack.

EPILOGUE

September 2012

I recently bought a small mirror. Since the encounter in the elevator in New York, I now come face to face with my own image often. Each morning, I do my long gray hair, a feminine gesture maybe. Then I wrap the fabric of my turban, a ritual for men that I carry out with precision from practice.

I have an appointment with the French journalists. They wanted to film me this time, but that is out of the question! My long hair, my feminine quality, is far too intimate! They want to make a documentary about the bacha posh. I did not know that this term was known outside of our country. They explained to me that there were other women like me, designated as boys from their birth, who refused to give up their male clothes at adolescence, as was expected of them. They had tasted the freedom of men and did not intend to abandon it. The American military, with whom I worked in Khost, took an interest in me; one thing led to another, and more journalists came to see me. Mostly Americans. And then somebody nominated me for the Most Courageous Woman of the Year award. This is how I found myself in the United States. It has not been easy, believe me, to make the district understand. "How dare you go there, you, who were in the jihad?"

Yes, America, today, is the enemy.

So here I am, a small celebrity and a great curiosity. And people ask me this question all the time: To be a bacha posh—is it a freedom or an imprisonment?

Here is my answer: Living in men's clothing has given me a certain freedom. A life as a woman in Afghanistan is a life of destruction. You saw where I come from, and where am I now? But I do not forget what I had to give up. For me, this is not a weight, to not get married, to not have children, to grow old alone . . . but, for others? I would not advise anyone to become a bacha posh.

If a little girl came to me and asked me for advice, I would say to her: I do not want to encourage you to wear men's clothing; this depends on your character and your courage. Look, there have been plenty of girls who dress themselves as boys, but they were not brave enough for it, and they stopped, and they had to learn how to become girls. They played soccer with the boys, they came and went as they pleased, and then, overnight, they put a veil on their heads and locked their hearts in a prison. They could no longer go out alone; they were expected to find husbands. Their universe is now a summation of whatever lies between the walls of their homes. This has been the case of the bacha posh in my village.

Then I would tell this little girl: If you continue to wear men's clothing, you must have the brave heart of a man, and the height. Men are strong and brave, sometimes unfair, and often cruel. Women have soft hearts; they cannot be like men. Me, I can be cruel when Satan takes hold of me. I have not killed anyone, but I can knock someone out. Therefore, I would say that everything depends on your heart and not on the garments. Abroad, I have seen women dressed in women's clothing who have brave hearts. They are fighting, they are working, they are strong. Therefore, dressing as a man is not the solution. Me, I had no choice. That is all there is to it; I could not do otherwise. My father said, "You will be a boy, my girl," and I have since remained a boy. In fact, I know that, at the bottom of me, that when he was pushing me to become his daughter, under the pressure of the mullahs, he was proud that I resisted. He had raised me that way; he made me a man.

But, you see, little girl, sometimes I think about death. And I know that I will be wrapped as a woman, because you can cheat everyone except Allah. The white sheet will overlap my head, and my hands will be laid on my chest. But in the next world, you see, I am going to ask Allah to make me a real woman or a real man. It is no big deal, but not half and half. Why? you ask. Because, without love and without desire, you sometimes feel lonely.